Getting *to the* Heart *of* Interfaith

The Eye-Opening, Hope-Filled Friendship of a Pastor, a Rabbi & a Sheikh

Pastor Don Mackenzie, Rabbi Ted Falcon
and Sheikh Jamal Rahman

Walking Together, Finding the Way®
SKYLIGHT PATHS®
PUBLISHING
Woodstock, Vermont

Getting to the Heart of Interfaith:
The Eye-Opening, Hope-Filled Friendship of a Pastor, a Rabbi and a Sheikh

2010 Quality Paperback Edition, Second Printing
2009 Quality Paperback Edition, First Printing
© 2009 by Don Mackenzie, Ted Falcon, and Jamal Rahman

Scripture quotations in Pastor Don Mackenzie's sections are from the *New Revised Standard Version Bible*, copyright © 1989 by the Division of Christian Education of the National Council of the Churches of Christ in the USA. Used by permission. All rights reserved.

Page 183 constitutes a continuation of this copyright page.

Library of Congress Cataloging-in-Publication Data
Mackenzie, Don, 1944–
  Getting to the heart of interfaith : the eye-opening, hope-filled friendship of a pastor, a rabbi, and a sheikh / by Don Mackenzie, Ted Falcon, and Jamal Rahman.
    p. cm.
  Includes bibliographical references.
  ISBN-13: 978-1-59473-263-8 (quality pbk.)
  ISBN-10: 1-59473-263-9 (quality pbk.)
  1. Religions—Relations. 2. Religious life. I. Falcon, Ted. II. Rahman, Jamal. III. Title.
  BL410.M26 2009
  201'.5—dc22

                                                              2009017114

10 9 8 7 6 5 4 3 2

Manufactured in the United States of America
Cover design: Tim Holtz
Cover art: Photo taken by Shira Firestone in 2007, at the radio studio of station KKNW of the Sandusky Radio Group in Bellevue, Washington.
The inside cover photo was taken by Jerry Pettitz in 2008 in Seattle, Washington.

SkyLight Paths is creating a place where people of different spiritual traditions come together for challenge and inspiration, a place where we can help each other understand the mystery that lies at the heart of our existence.

SkyLight Paths sees both believers and seekers as a community that increasingly transcends traditional boundaries of religion and denomination—people wanting to learn from each other, *walking together, finding the way.*

SkyLight Paths, "Walking Together, Finding the Way," and colophon are trademarks of LongHill Partners, Inc., registered in the U.S. Patent and Trademark Office.

Walking Together, Finding the Way®
Published by SkyLight Paths Publishing
A Division of LongHill Partners, Inc.
Sunset Farm Offices, Route 4, P.O. Box 237
Woodstock, VT 05091
Tel: (802) 457-4000 Fax: (802) 457-4004
www.skylightpaths.com

To Father William Treacy
and to the memory of
Rabbi Raphael Levine
with deep appreciation and affection.

They opened the heart of Seattle to interfaith with their
television program *Challenge*, which aired from 1960–1974,
and in 1968, they founded Camp Brotherhood, a major
interfaith retreat center in the Pacific Northwest.

Contents

Introduction

It's a matter of our survival.

We will survive only if we learn to treat ourselves, our neighbors, and our planet with greater wisdom, compassion, and caring. We will survive only if we learn to replace the current climate—of fragmentation, suspicion, and self-interest that has our planet warming, countries warring, and loving relationships waning—with more hopeful visions.

In our own day, it appears that religions are at the heart of some of the world's most brutal conflicts. Religion seems to be fueling hatred rather than expanding love. Each religion seems to be projecting a God in its own image, interpreting ancient words through its own filters. What was meant to unite is used to divide. This is the challenge of interfaith dialogue and collaboration.

The expansive perspective we seek is called *inclusive spirituality*. We believe that this inclusive spiritual awareness holds the key to the healing for which we yearn as individuals, as couples, as families, as countries, and as peoples. We believe that this more inclusive awareness will allow us to heal the wounds experienced by both person and planet.

Look around you. We are living in a pluralistic world society. While we might not talk about it much, we usually interact each day with those of different cultures and different religions. What we have found is that *not* talking about our differences really does not help. Even if we differ, even if we disagree, it is crucial for us to deepen the conversation. We are hoping to bring you into the conversation that we three have been sharing as a pastor, a rabbi, and a sheikh, and we are hoping to inspire you to engage in your own conversations with those of different faiths around you.

One of the difficulties, of course, is that conflicts tend to arise among people of different belief systems. You might wonder, for example, particularly when beliefs differ significantly, whether there is any way for both beliefs to be "right." Is there one truth? Is there one right way? These are just a few of the questions that come up when we begin creating dialogue in our pluralistic society.

We want to elevate the conversation to a spiritual level so that we can perceive more clearly how different belief systems can, in fact, lead to the same place. We also want to elevate the conversation because this is a path to greater peace in our personal lives and in the life of our world. While disagreements and differing beliefs may support the existence of different communities and cultures, that which is shared is more universal. It is our intention in *Getting to the Heart of Interfaith* to celebrate the shared healing wisdom, compassion, and vitality at the heart of the three Abrahamic faiths.

We believe that an inclusive spirituality holds a key to the healing that needs to take place in our day. By its very nature, inclusive spirituality embraces differences and makes no demand that we all believe the same things. It takes us beyond our particular beliefs into shared values of love, compassion, and peace toward which we all are striving. None of us can get there alone—we absolutely need each other to heal the global problems that we are facing.

If you are concerned about the deeper healing of people and our planet, and if you realize that we must find ways of entering into conversation with those different from us, then this book is for you. As we share some of the challenges we have faced over the years we have worked together, you may well recognize issues in your own life. Perhaps our insights will inspire you to embrace more hopeful perspectives, based on the ways that we have found to deal with our own conflicts and concerns.

This book is grounded in the spirit of healing. We believe that true healing comes when we are able to transcend the suffering and pain, and embrace them from a more expansive perspective. This healing perspective exists within all spiritual paths. Reclaiming this teaching is the promise of interfaith dialogue, collaboration, and celebration.

There are five stages of the interfaith journey that we will highlight in particular: moving beyond separation and suspicion, inquiring more deeply, sharing both the easy and the difficult parts, moving beyond safe territory, and exploring spiritual practices from other traditions. Through sharing our stories, beliefs, and practices, which are of profound importance to us, we will walk you through our experience of these stages. As you read our stories, you may find parallels in your own life. You may remember dramas that are ready to be shared, ready to be healed, ready to be celebrated.

Before you start, we think it is crucial to point out that interfaith dialogue and interfaith celebration are *not* about conversion. In fact, our experience has been just the opposite. Each of the three of us continues to experience a deepening of our roots in our own faith tradition as these roots are nurtured by wisdom teachings of other traditions. We feel more complete in our spiritual identities because of our sharing.

We hope that *Getting to the Heart of Interfaith* inspires you to risk the next step in your spiritual journey and to create spaces for greater dialogue and deeper celebration in your life and in your community. We encourage you to use the Discussion Questions at the back of the book to spur your thinking, to talk with your faith community or interfaith group, and to take action in the world.

As we strive to appreciate both the blessings and the griefs of each of our faiths, we dedicate ourselves to envisioning together a world of greater understanding, acceptance, compassion, and love. We dream of a world awakening to the essential Oneness that contains us all.

1
THE INTERFAITH JOURNEY

Stages of Interfaith Dialogue and Collaboration

What Is Interfaith?

The word *interfaith* has become somewhat of a buzzword these days, and interfaith services are becoming more and more common. But many such efforts get stalled after a few token meetings and a few initial forays into interfaith territory because people are at a loss. Perhaps the gatherings feel superficial, or people encounter differences that seem insurmountable. Or maybe they aren't quite sure what the purpose is or don't know what to do next. They may like the "idea" of interfaith, but have only a vague sense of what that might entail.

Since we're going to be taking an interfaith journey together in this book, we want to be clear at the outset about what we mean by *interfaith* and how it is different from some other terms floating around, such as *interreligious* and *interspiritual*. It appears that *interfaith* is a relatively recent word, most likely coined between 1965 and 1970. Dictionaries say it is an adjective, relating to some kind of activity or relationship between people of different religions, though we take it a step further, according it the status of a noun as well. We would expand that meaning a little because there are some faith traditions that do not consider themselves to be "religions," and we would also wish to include those who are not members of any particular faith tradition. *Interfaith*, then, in our view, points toward activities or relationships between people with different beliefs or faith identities. Sometimes the difference between people within a particular faith tradition is so great that we might even see a relationship between them as an "interfaith" relationship. (Of course, to be more precise, such a relationship would fall under the term *intrafaith*.)

People often use the terms *interreligious* and *interfaith* interchangeably, but it seems to us that interreligious is used most properly when talking about the activities or relationships between or among different religious institutions. Sometimes we hear the word *interspiritual*, an even more recently coined term, as a way of extracting the spiritual dimensions from the rest of a faith or a nonfaith tradition.

Even the word *faith* has different layers of meaning. In Christianity, faith deals more specifically with belief. When Pastor Don uses the word *faith*, he is talking about a way of understanding experience that is grounded in a trust in God, a trust that gives us what we need to cooperate with God's purposes, to do God's will. For him, *faith* means seeing things as Don Quixote saw the barmaid Aldonzo Lorenzo as his lovely Lady Dulcinea—through eyes of love. Christians see life through eyes of faith.

When Rabbi Ted uses the Hebrew word *emunah*, which is often translated as "faith," it signifies firmness and is related more to action than to belief. This firmness indicates a kind of faithfulness in the sense of reliability, and can be translated as "It is so-ness." *Emunah* is from the same word root as *amen*, which means, "It is so."

When Sheikh Jamal uses the word *faith*, he is referring to the Qur'an's teaching, which specifies that a Muslim must build faith in God, angels, prophets, holy books, and the Day of Judgment. In these five beliefs, the devotee must move from "borrowed certainty" to what the Holy Book calls "inner certainty." There is a story of an exchange between a Bedouin and the Prophet Muhammad that highlights this essential trust. When the Bedouin asked, "Should I tether my camel to the post or trust in God alone?" the Prophet replied, "First, tether the camel and then trust in God."

To be sure, the United States as a world culture is at the very beginning of our understanding of what interfaith is and what it can contribute to the common good. So far, in our journey together, we three have discovered that it helps to identify the universals—such as love, peace, compassion, and justice—that transcend the boundaries of our different traditions. Interfaith exploration helps us identify the particulars within our own faith traditions that support those universals—as well as the particulars that do not support those universals. This, then, has become an invitation for each of us to gain a deeper understanding of our own traditions while, at the same time, listening to each other describe similar aspects of their traditions. We are certain that this kind of interfaith exchange could lead to a level of cooperation and collaboration among the peoples of the world that has never happened before.

The question is this: How to get from here to there? From our experience together as a Christian, a Jew, and a Muslim, we have identified some key stages that we hope can help you identify where you are on the interfaith journey and understand how you can move forward.

Five Stages on the Interfaith Journey

The three of us are an unlikely trio: Don Mackenzie is a pastor; Ted Falcon, a rabbi; and Jamal Rahman, a sheikh. We have been called the "Interfaith Amigos," but getting to this point—learning from each other, understanding our differences, working through the difficult matters, and forging a genuine friendship—has been an eye-opening journey over the span of many years.

As we continue to discover the deeper dimensions of our interfaith journey, and as we meet with others who are active in interfaith organizations and efforts, one of the things that has become clear to us is that we all go through similar stages to get to the point where interfaith dialogue, collaboration, and celebration become possible. Our experience has been that there are essentially five stages on the interfaith journey:

Stage 1: Moving beyond separation and suspicion
Stage 2: Inquiring more deeply
Stage 3: Sharing both the easy and the difficult parts
Stage 4: Moving beyond safe territory
Stage 5: Exploring spiritual practices from other traditions

We invite you to come along with us as we dip into the stories of our experience of these stages. Perhaps you will recognize yourself, either as you were or as you are, or as you might like to become. Whatever stage you find yourself in, know that each stage represents an important part of an ongoing process of getting to the heart of interfaith.

Stage 1: Moving Beyond Separation and Suspicion

At the outset of any attempt at interfaith dialogue or collaboration, it is important to recognize that there may be—in fact, probably will be—issues that have the potential to divide people into different camps, even to polarize interfaith work before it gets off the ground. There may be preconceived notions about what people think and believe that make us suspicious or fearful or critical of each other.

Separation and suspicion can be subtle; they can crop up when you least expect them. We remember well the time when Jamal was invited to present a Qur'an to the interfaith chapel of Camp Brotherhood, where we have served as board members, frequent presenters, and sponsors of interfaith programs. The chapel already housed an ornate Bible and a narrow ark containing a surprisingly large Torah scroll, and we believed that the inclusion of the Qur'an in a public event would demonstrate in a concrete way the inclusiveness that Camp Brotherhood exemplified. We designed a simple and sacred ceremony, set a date, and felt blessed by the response from the enthusiastic invitees. However, just a few days before the event, some members of the Camp Brotherhood board objected, saying they would not be comfortable placing the Qur'an in the chapel. In order to appear tolerant, the board decided that the Torah and the Bible would be taken out of the chapel, and could be joined by the Qur'an in a museum-type setting to be created beneath the chapel.

We were disappointed, but we accepted this situation as a sign that deeper dialogue was needed; more bridges needed to be built. We had hoped that such a moment could become an opening rather than a closing. In some very frank discussions with members of the board, a few admitted they were fearful that if the Qur'an were in the chapel, "ordinary" Christians and Jews would refuse to use the place. We thanked them for their willingness to express their belief and gently explained, to the best of our abilities, how central it was to the mission of Camp Brotherhood to build awareness, respond to fears, and demonstrate the willingness and courage to engage with each other and make changes.

Our conversations and relationships had already produced changes, and our aspiration is that, with continued dialogue, friendship, and allaying of fears, the three sacred books of the Abrahamic faiths will eventually find their way together into the sanctuary.

Getting to know each other builds tolerance, and telling each other our stories is where this begins. When we share vignettes from our childhood, tales of how we grew up, experiences that shaped our lives, excitement about what interests us, we are building the bridges that can carry us past separation and suspicion.

Our personal stories begin to make connections that are more powerful than suspicion and distrust.

People of different faiths might be our neighbors, but we know very little about each other. We might work in the same place, but be virtual strangers. Talking about matters of faith is most unusual in ordinary, day-to-day living. Most of us would say that we respect each other's religions, but the reality is that we probably don't know very much about each other—let alone each other's faiths.

This presents us with an opportunity—and a challenge. How can we get to know each other? What do we need to do to put ourselves in a place where an exchange of stories can happen?

The three of us had been presenting interfaith programs together for several years when we began to realize that we needed to reach out more actively to those who were indifferent or opposed to interfaith efforts. We were grateful for the turnout at our programs, but we knew that we were often preaching to the choir. Whenever there was a major interfaith event in the city, we were frequently among the "usual suspects" who led the program. But also among the attendees, whether it was fifty or five hundred, we began to see the same faces over and over again. We were deeply grateful for their loyalty, but where were the conservative Christians, Jews, or Muslims? How could we include them as program leaders and participants? It became amply clear to us after a few creative attempts to include them that they would not come to us. We had to go to them. We knew we had to start by getting acquainted, so they could get to know us, and we them. On one particular foray into a large megachurch of evangelical Christians in Seattle, we were in for a few surprises.

AN EVANGELICAL ADVENTURE. Eager to explore ways to connect with this rapidly growing community, two of us, Rabbi Ted and Sheikh Jamal, joined a small interfaith delegation to visit a very popular Seattle church one Sunday morning. The church's "protocol officer" gave us a gracious tour of the extensive campus, which also housed a K-12 school, a university and a nearby helicopter pad to carry the minister to the church's second facility north of Seattle. We were struck by the informality and hospitality of the rather vast main building, with its lounging areas of comfortable sofas, espresso service, and snack bars. When we entered the giant sanctuary, holding what would be some five thousand people, we saw that the congregation was surprisingly diverse, and a significant number were minorities: African-Americans, Hispanics, and Samoans.

The music suddenly blasted us into a different space. Six singers and a full band launched into several powerful church numbers with great joy. The words appeared on the two huge screens bracketing the stage, and all of us sang along. The noise was loud enough that there was little danger anyone that would be bothered as we mangled the melodies but joined right in.

Finally, the flamboyant and youthful-looking pastor began his sermon. We felt the intensity of his passion and were a little surprised at the spiritual teaching he was sharing. Continuously invoking Jesus, he proclaimed a message of love and caring that was not what we had been expecting. We got to examine some of our own prejudices that morning, since we had anticipated a far more particularistic sermon. In example after example, he exhorted his flock to be like Jesus. "If an unwed mother becomes pregnant," he said, "be like Jesus: Help her, don't condemn her. If a gay person contracts AIDS, don't be quick to judge. Be like Jesus: Be quick to help this person. There is no need to look at their backgrounds. There is no need to look at their past behavior." At one point Ted nudged Jamal to whisper jokingly that this was so good that it was disappointing!

Then, as if on cue so he would not disappoint us, the pastor paused dramatically in the midst of this outpouring of unalloyed love and burst out, "But if you want an angry God, be a Muslim! If you want to be someone who is filled with hate, rage, and destruction, be a Muslim!" Rabbi Ted was aghast and felt protective of Sheikh Jamal, but Jamal actually welcomed this assertion because this gave him an opening to talk about something substantive with the pastor. Jamal saw this as an opportunity to share and get to know the pastor on a more personal level.

We met with the pastor after the service, exchanged pleasantries, and then Jamal began to talk about the special place in which Jesus is held in Muslim tradition. It was clear that the pastor had little awareness of this aspect of Islam. It took a while, but the mood began to change. Jamal's communication created a bridge where none had existed before. Jamal was delighted with the pastor's willingness to appreciate that the traditions of Islam taught the very same lessons about love and compassion that the pastor's own teachings conveyed.

We didn't know what the greater consequences of that conversation would be, but those moments of dialogue created a meaningful connection between the pastor's Christianity and the teachings of Islam. The person-to-person conversation allowed a previously held stereotype to be released.

In a meeting some weeks later, the pastor was polite but frank. He explained that he was so busy with his expanding church that he had no urgent need to connect or work with clergy or congregations of other faiths. Besides, he confided, his congregants would wind up wanting to convert every one of us to Christianity.

We joked that we welcomed their prayers and encouraged him to explore avenues of collaboration. We emphasized the reality that in a pluralistic society we have to find ways to get beyond our separation, to coexist. If there is to be a solution to the problems of poverty, homelessness, and global warming, it will take all of us working together. In the end, he did agree to have one of the church's social action groups join us in a project involving social justice or earth care. Though his church had its own community outreach programs, he was willing to collaborate on a social issue in a limited way.

In later conversations with that social action committee, we agreed to work together on an Interfaith Habitat for Humanity project in West Seattle, where congregations of various faiths would join hands to build homes for low-income families. In a fine bit of poetic justice, the beneficiary of this particular project happened to be a Muslim family. This project is going on as we write this. Our understanding is that those involved are not spending much time talking about their respective faiths; they are focused on learning to handle tools!

But this is a good start. When people work together on a project, they begin to see each other as "persons," not as "Jews" or "Christians" or "Muslims." And from there, it becomes natural to share a few stories about their lives, to exchange information about their families and kids, to share concerns about the local school, and so forth. And who knows where all this "getting acquainted" might lead? Perhaps it will be the beginning of what might develop into deeper levels of more knowledgeable tolerance. Perhaps it will be the beginning of some new friendships. Ultimately, sharing each other's stories, getting to know each other, is the first and best way to begin to move beyond separation and suspicion.

Stage 2: Inquiring More Deeply

As the process of interfaith dialogue evolves, people naturally begin to inquire more deeply about the specifics of each other's approaches to God, ways of worship, and sacred rituals of celebration. What do "they" believe? What are their faith traditions? Mahatma Gandhi often emphasized in his talks that to cultivate peace in a multireligious society, it is a sacred duty of every individual to have an appreciative understanding of other people's traditions. And, as we have found, the paradoxical nature of this stage is that it leads us not only to learn about other traditions, but requires us to delve more deeply into our own.

Interfaith worship can be a good vehicle for moving toward a greater awareness of different faith traditions, allowing us to worship God and deepen an appreciative understanding of the basic teachings of each other's faiths. We wanted to go beyond simply having a minister, a rabbi, or a sheikh deliver sermons in each other's pulpits. We wanted a service created by people of different faiths. Although each of our traditions is distinct, we realized that there are some commonalities about the rhythm of our worship services, so we tried distributing these sections among different faith leaders. This helped to focus the worship experience, to make it feel more whole.

Yet the interest and excitement began to wear thin for us, and we finally figured out that it was richer when we had one main service leader and tradition, to which others could provide enrichment. It was in this context that we found we could learn more fully and experience more deeply each other's faiths. We now avoid the need to provide "equal time" for each and allow ourselves to more clearly support each other. This has worked out to be a framework for interfaith worship that has enabled us to honor and more deeply appreciate each of our faiths.

There are many ways of sharing core beliefs that can lead to an appreciation of another's faith. Sometimes simply being in the presence of someone who is practicing their deeply rooted faith is much more powerful than all the words and services and sermons we could plan. We discovered this dimension through a very special sharing of Shabbat in a tiny apartment in the mystical city of Sfat in northern Israel.

AN ULTRA-ORTHODOX SHABBAT IN SFAT. When the three of us decided to lead an interfaith journey to Israel and Palestine (which we'll discuss in greater depth in chapter 5), Rabbi Ted called his nephew, Yonah Akiba, who is a member of an ultra-Orthodox community in the city of Sfat. On previous trips, Rabbi Ted had joined Yonah for Shabbat worship and then dinner, and Ted wanted to share that experience with Sheikh Jamal and Pastor Don.

Ted broached the subject with Yonah, who responded that he would have to talk with his rabbi. No one in his community had ever had a Muslim to their home, and he needed to make sure that was acceptable.

Permission was granted, and on the second Shabbat of the trip we traveled to Sfat for dinner. Though we arrived too late for worship, we met Yonah as he walked from the synagogue to his apartment. A slight man in his early thirties, he wore the long, dark-blue coat identifying him as a member of his Bratzlaver community—followers of Rabbi Nachman of Bratzlav, who lived in the latter part of the eighteenth century. Because it was Shabbat, his black hat was replaced by a *shtreiml,* a very special hat with a ring of rich fur around the sides.

At his apartment, we were greeted by his wife, Rivka Sarah, and their sons, who love to have company for Shabbat. Though Yonah lives very simply, and his life is devoted to study and to teaching, somehow there is always enough money for a Shabbat feast.

Yonah began with the traditional blessing over the wine, his eyes half-closed, his body rocking rhythmically as he slowly chanted the words. It seemed to us that each word was an offering of holiness, sanctifying the moment we shared. We were struck by the depth of his devotion in preparation for the Shabbat meal. After the wine was passed around to all of us, Yonah took two challahs, the special braided breads for Shabbat, and cut them to dip into the salt on the plate. Reminiscent of the ancient Temple offerings, the salted bread was held aloft as we shared the blessing and then the bread. The glow on Yonah's and Rivka Sarah's faces added to the joy of the moment. It was as if we were sharing a little piece of paradise in a small, unassuming apartment in the Galilee. It was home.

Our paths are very different. They did not have an interest in our interfaith work and perceived no benefit in expanding the dialogue with others; they saw their responsibility as preserving their particular traditions. Yet we were able to appreciate how deeply devoted Yonah and his family were to living their faith. Certainly, Don and Jamal had never encountered this traditional aspect of Judaism before (Ted wears black much of the time, but it's more of a fashion statement than religious garb).

We also understood that if we were to truly appreciate each other, then we must also accept that many would not be open to the interfaith spiritual journey that the three of us share. That evening together was wonderful, not because we all agreed with each other, but because we sat together with open hearts. We would like to think that this dinner accomplished more than breaking the "Muslim barrier" in that household and in that community. We would like to think that there are reverberations for all of us that will support the greater peace we all are seeking.

It is also clear to us that inquiring more deeply into the teachings of another faith and acquiring an appreciative understanding of that faith does not simply mean gathering facts about that faith tradition. It also means beginning to get a feeling for the depth of relationship between a person and that person's faith tradition. If we cannot start learning to do that, we will remain stuck judging the other's faith by the reality of our own. We say "start learning" because we cannot ever totally know what is in another person's heart. What is important is our willingness to understand. This will make us less judgmental, more sympathetic, and willing to cooperate more fully with each other.

Stage 3: Sharing Both the Easy and the Difficult Parts

It would be nice if our traditions consistently taught the messages of compassion and love that are reflected through every page of our holy books. But that is simply not the case. Every religion, Gandhi taught, has its truths and its untruths—especially your own. Jamal insists that Gandhi winked as he spoke the last words of that teaching, but it often seems to us that the winking is Jamal's! Yet the teaching speaks to a distinction that each of us needs to become more aware of: the contrast between the universal teachings and the more time-bound verses of our traditions.

Rabbi Ted looks at the violence in the Hebrew Bible as examples of this kind of time-bound teaching. Pastor Don views the anti-Jewish aspects of his tradition in that same light. But, because of the current political situation, it is Sheikh Jamal who most often must respond to accusations regarding the violence taught in the Qur'an.

We can no longer count the number of times he has been challenged to explain the Islamic teachings of jihad. From Jamal's point of view, *jihad* refers primarily to an exertion of spiritual energies; it refers to a person's engagement on the spiritual path. But there is no denying that some of the teachings of the Qur'an have been utilized by more militant groups to support their political agendas rather than their spiritual paths.

Admitting the perceived imperfections—and the real dissonances we struggle with—in our spiritual traditions is not an easy thing to do, especially to someone outside our tradition. Yet this is an important step on the interfaith journey if we are to reach a place of deeper and more honest dialogue. When we can be candid about both what we love about our faiths, and where we have the most discomfort, we offer each other not only the gift of openness but also the gift of a deeper understanding about ourselves and what matters most to us. In addition, the acknowledgment of what troubles us about our own faith may open new opportunities to probe further into what we truly believe, as it did for Pastor Don one particular Easter season.

DID THE JEWS KILL JESUS? In the spring of 2006, Don invited Ted, his wife Ruth, Jamal, and members of their communities to join his congregation for the celebration of Maundy Thursday. Since all three congregations had shared a Passover seder the previous year, he thought it fitting to invite them to the Christian observance of the Last Supper, which was likely a form of a seder meal that Jesus shared with his disciples the night before his execution.

When Don looked over the Maundy Thursday readings, however, he was struck by the degree to which the blame for Jesus's death was freely ascribed to the Jews. He knew these verses had prompted much hatred and violence toward the Jewish people over many centuries, and he was inspired to look more deeply into the essential meaning of Maundy Thursday.

Don saw that the word *Maundy* comes from the Latin *mandatum,* meaning "commandment." So he focused on the idea that Maundy Thursday reminds us of Jesus's commandment that we love one another, as he loved us. Don then arranged the readings to eliminate those that contributed to anti-Jewish sentiments and added others more pertinent to the spiritual meaning of Maundy Thursday.

The harder part for Don was that the problematic readings existed at all. References to the Jews in the Gospels are often negative and are made without reference to the fact that Jesus and his followers were all Jews. The Gospels seem to forget that the Jews were under the occupation of the Romans and therefore without the power needed to condemn someone to death. In truth, many Jews were crucified in those years, but Jews themselves never crucified anyone. These verses are difficult and, for Don, constituted an untruth in the Christian tradition.

We cannot deny these "shadow sides" of our sacred literatures; they are clear reflections of the shadow side of our own personalities. It is crucial for each of us to admit that our traditions, while mostly focused on paths toward a shared Universal, also reflect more narrow concerns. As we can more openly share these problem texts and problematic interpretations, our interfaith dialogue can deepen, and our understanding and appreciation of our own faith can grow.

Stage 4: Moving Beyond Safe Territory

Safe territory constitutes that which is familiar to us and also meets the approval of the groups and institutions we belong to. We humans are strongly inclined to conform to opinions and models of behavior sanctioned by our particular communities. Consciously or subconsciously, we tend to move toward those whose thinking and ways of being are similar to ours. Meeting those whose ways of thinking and being are different can be challenging. What allows us to move beyond safe territory? Perhaps it is our awareness that we are all part of something larger.

All relationships provide contexts for growing, and growing always includes challenges. From those challenges, our relationships either dissolve or grow stronger. There have been times when differences between Jamal and Ted have become pointed. Perhaps because of the strength of their relationship, those differences have provided grist for the mill of deeper dialogue.

It is no surprise that one of those difficult issues focused on the relationship between the State of Israel and the surrounding Arab nations. Rabbi Ted commented during one of our Interfaith Talk Radio shows that Israel was a tiny, vulnerable state surrounded by the might of Arab countries. Israel is 1/640th the landmass of the surrounding Arab states and would fit into the state of Florida seven times. As Pastor Don moderated the conversation, it became clear that, for Jamal, the picture was quite different. Sheikh Jamal explained that Israel loomed larger for the surrounding Arab countries, partly because of Israel's military might and partly because they always perceived Israel and the United States as one unit. It took Ted some time to be able to grasp Jamal's perception, since it seemed so diametrically opposed to Ted's reality. Once he was able to hear what Jamal shared, however, it became easier to continue dialogue on matters of the Middle East. Similarly for Jamal, once he was able to truly listen to Ted's concerns and Don's moderation of the conversation, both his understanding and his empathy grew for Ted's point of view.

We three have discovered that one of the consequences of moving beyond safe territory is the ability to expand our points of view. We don't have all the answers, of course, but we know that our dialogue is certainly the beginning of the healing that needs to take place. We experienced this in a very direct way on our interfaith trip to Israel and Palestine.

ON ALIEN GROUND. We visited *Yad Vashem*, the Holocaust memorial, and the very next day went to the newly walled city of Bethlehem on the West Bank. We anguished at both those places. We did not equate them in any sense, but each of those days invited us to recognize deep levels of deprivation and human suffering. Both experiences challenged us to understand what it felt like to be the other.

The unspeakable magnitude of pain honored at the Holocaust memorial took our breath away. The monumental nature of the Nazis' attempt to eradicate the Jewish people pierced our hearts. And there was a special dimension of challenge for Don and the other non-Jewish members of the group who, to one degree or another, identified with the Christian perpetrators of that horror. For a while, most of us were unable to talk about the feelings awakened in us and what the dramatic juxtaposition of the visits had done to us.

We all felt the desolation and economic struggles in Bethlehem, where unemployment is skyrocketing and the occupation clearly has a depressing effect on the residents. Rabbi Ted and some of the Jews in our group felt special pain because they also identified with those who had built the wall that separated Bethlehem from Israel and marginalized the Palestinian people.

We didn't really come to grips with those experiences until several days later. We found ourselves visiting the ruins of a Roman metropolis called Tsippori, the ancient city of Sephorus. At the time of Jesus, Nazareth was a kind of suburb to Sephorus. In a large open-air theater, we wound up gathering and finally talking as a group about our experiences at the Holocaust Memorial and Bethlehem.

In the chilly afternoon air, we shared our anguish. We had no real "answers" but could hear each other's pain. We all shared aspects of both the victims and the victimizers. We realized how our religious traditions could be used to cause great pain to the other.

We had ventured into some very difficult territory and, in the end, we shared spaces of silence that held some of the healing we were seeking. But it was a shared silence in which we experienced each other's support. The inner and outer territory we experienced was beyond our safety zones, yet we found ourselves more tightly bound as an interfaith community because of it.

Stage 5: Exploring Spiritual Practices from Other Traditions

The three of us once spoke during a Sunday service at the Fauntleroy United Church of Christ in Seattle, and one of the topics we touched on was the value of experiencing spiritual practices of other traditions. In the question-and-answer period, a Jewish visitor shared that he once was surprised to see two Muslim men in a restroom prayerfully focused on a purification ritual with water. With great care, they washed their hands, elbows, rinsed their nostrils, cleaned their ears, splashed their faces and eyes, ran their damp hands over their hair and neck and washed their feet. With each cleansing motion, they said something. He learned that they were preparing themselves for the body prayer and that the soft intoning were internal prayers, such as "May these hands always be of service to You, my Cherisher and Sustainer" to accompany the washing of hands; or a more specific prayer to follow the cleansing of the ears: "May I refuse to listen to gossip." As that man witnessed them with fascination, he felt a palpable shift in himself. His understanding and appreciation of Islamic body prayers inspired him to say his own Jewish prayers with a deeper sense of purification and presence.

The idea of exploring practices of other faiths is not to judge or compare them but to experience the beauty of the same Spirit that pervades all spiritual practices. Sometimes a spiritual practice of another tradition can touch us so deeply that we want to weave it in into our own. Treasures from another's faith practice can supplement our own practices and help us grow during our spiritual journey.

By entering into this kind of experience of the heart, we can soften our fear of what is unfamiliar and different. This journey has its ups and downs. The path is not easy, but the rewards are beautiful. By exploring each other's spiritual practices, we can begin to cultivate an inner spaciousness that allows us to embrace and celebrate the different forms of religious experience so we can discover the universals we share.

As we "Interfaith Amigos" began to learn more about each other's faith practices, we often looked for occasions to participate in each other's religious services and rituals and spiritual practices. In particular, we were able to explore the interfaith dimensions of seder and Ramadan, to "try on" each other's spiritual practices in a way that honored the authenticity of the experience while, at the same time, giving each of us a chance to see where the practice touched our own hearts. For more than five years, Christians, Jews, and Muslims in our congregations have celebrated seder and Ramadan together in Seattle.

INTERFAITH DIMENSIONS OF SEDER. The coming of spring can bring a sense of rebirth, a sense of being renewed, even transformed. So it is not surprising that religious traditions have developed spring holidays to help channel that energy in spiritual ways. In Jewish tradition, the spring festival is Passover.

When Rabbi Ted invites Pastor Don and Sheikh Jamal to participate in his congregation's celebration of Passover, that doesn't make it an interfaith seder. It is an authentic Jewish celebration of Passover in which leaders from Islam and Christianity have the opportunity to add teachings that focus on the major themes of Passover. It is interfaith in its constituency, but Jewish in its liturgy, its story, and its music.

Passover is the holiday celebrating the Jewish Exodus from ancient Egypt. Each year, Jews are challenged to live into this story by refraining from eating leavened products during the week of Passover. Unleavened bread, called matzah, recalls this ancient journey when, because of their haste, no time was available for the bread to rise. Matzah is also a symbol of a simpler way of life—it is made of only flour and water—and Passover is a time for returning to the basics of the spiritual path.

During the Passover ritual, the text of the Haggadah, the traditional telling of the ancient enslavement first to idolatry and then later to the Egyptians, is recited in Jewish homes all over the world. Because the Hebrew word for Egypt, *Mitzrayim,* signifies "places of stuckness," the Passover rituals have come to focus on the ways in which people have become stuck in their lives, enslaved to habits of thought and action, and to cultures of violence and war. Just as redemption came to their Jewish ancestors, at each seder Jews seek ways to release themselves from their present enslavements, from their current places of stuckness.

The word *seder* itself refers to the "order" of the symbolic meal and provides the context for remembering and for celebrating. Because the Exodus was the critical event in Jewish history that brought the Jewish people into being, the holiday is observed at home or in larger community settings.

As Pastor Don participated in the service, he helped us discover the parallels between the Passover and Holy Week stories, since Jesus's last week in Jerusalem was during the observance of Passover. On the Sunday that Jesus came into Jerusalem, he entered a place of multiple dimensions of imprisonment—the Roman occupation and the collaboration of the Temple bureaucracy with the occupying forces. As the week progressed, those "stuck places," along with the fear they inspired, led to Judas's betrayal of Jesus, Peter's denial of his relationship to Jesus, and even to the crucifixion that seemed to undermine hopes for transformation.

Whether understood literally or metaphorically, or both, res-urrection and the Exodus from Egypt have many parallels. Both speak of a freedom beyond what human hands can create, and for-giveness from a loving God who can make us new people. In these parallels, Pastor Don found his understanding of his own tradition deepened through the seder ritual.

For Jamal, the interfaith seder was in joyous alignment with both the letter and spirit of the Qur'an. The themes of seder—slavery, redemption, freedom, and guidance from God—are also an integral part of the spiritual journey of Islam. The word *Islam* means to surrender to God in peace, and the path of Islam involves the difficult but essential work of freeing oneself from the slavery of the ego, the "commanding master," as it is commonly described by Sufis, so that one can "bring a heart turned in devotion to God" (50:33).

Jamal offered the insight that the stories of the Exodus shared in the seder are reminders that freedom from the slavery of the ego is difficult. But the seder celebration inspires us always to seek God's help because, "the Guidance of God—that is the only Guidance" (2:120). And, as the Prophet Muhammad added, if we take one step toward the All-Compassionate God, God takes seven steps toward us; walk in the direction of God, and God comes to us running.

For all three of us, this sharing allowed us to reinforce and to celebrate our shared journey. We witnessed how each tradition responds to basic human challenges we all experience. Through this celebration, we were enriched as human beings, and we were confirmed as well in the deepening of our faith identities.

INTERFAITH DIMENSIONS OF RAMADAN AND ISLAMIC PRAYERS. To express gratitude to God for the gift of the Qur'an, Muslims com-memorate the month in which the first verses descended on the Prophet Muhammad. This observance, called Ramadan, takes place during the ninth month (also named Ramadan) of the Islamic lunar calendar and is one of the five pillars of Islam. During this month of spiritual purification, Muslims fast from sunrise to sunset and renew their commitments to surrender to God and to be of service to God's creation.

During Ramadan, breaking of the fast with food and drink at dusk each evening is meant to be gratefully shared in community, with family and friends, and also with strangers. Since 9/11, it has become a tradition in many cities in America for mosques and Muslim homes to open their doors to people of different faiths to share in the break-fast, called *Iftar*. At the same time, many churches, synagogues, and other houses of worship have graciously invited Muslims to share *Iftar* with their congregations.

Over the years since 9/11, Jamal's and Ted's and Don's congregations have shared food, reflections, and worship during Ramadan numerous times. Besides the sense of joyous community that is created, this coming together during *Iftar* is a wonderful occasion for non-Muslims to learn about the spiritual meaning of Ramadan, and for Muslims to become aware, from Christian and Jewish speakers, of fasting experiences during Lent and Yom Kippur. For Jamal, it is deeply moving when, following the breaking of the fast, Christians, Jews, and people of other faiths stand shoulder to shoulder and bow, kneel, and prostrate themselves with their Muslim brothers and sisters in the evening prayers.

Traditionally, Muslims pray five times a day, praising and thanking God, using the gift of the body to express this adoration and gratitude. For both Ted and Don—once they got past the awkwardness of learning the movements—bowing together in unison to the same God brought an exquisite sense of humility and community. And they are not alone. Jamal shared a story of several women who commented that they felt as if they were on a "divine date with God" and have chosen to incorporate this prostration prayer into their Christian practices.

As the three of us contemplated the meaning of these sacred body prayers, Jamal told us a lovely story that the sage Rumi told about a mother who makes cookies out of dough and sugar and shapes them into different animals. The children shout and fight excitedly over the fish, lion, and camel cookies, but the mother knows that as the children eat them, the cookies turn into the same sweetness inside the mouth. This is the true hope and promise of interfaith collaboration: the more we can share in each other's spiritual practices, the more we can savor the "sweetness" of each other's traditions.

The Next Step

As you consider these five stages of interfaith exploration, you may discover that you have experienced some of them already. Different people will find themselves at different places along this path. Beware of judgments concerning how far you have come. Being on the way is far more important than getting to the final stage. We all, at various times, take at least one step back for every step forward. But every step forward is a step in courage, and a step in trust. So be encouraged, and celebrate each new stage as you meet and embrace it.

We invite you to think about what faith means for you and to consider the hope that we believe lives inside the promise of interfaith. We encourage you to share your faith journey with someone from another tradition and to ask them about theirs. If you'd like to explore aspects of your faith that make you uncomfortable or to move beyond safe territory, we suggest that you do it with someone you trust. And as you begin to experiment with spiritual practices from other traditions, we celebrate with you!

2

THE POWER OF OUR STORIES

Moving Beyond Separation and Suspicion

Interfaith from the Inside Out

When we meet a stranger for the first time, some of us are shy and quiet, while others jump in and shake hands or give hugs and start talking. A lot depends on our personalities. But a lot also depends on our unspoken perceptions of the other person, especially if we've been told they come from a place or a group we don't know much about or don't understand. We might be curious, but we might be equally intimidated, or even suspicious. All we know is that they're "different" from us. Striking up a conversation may be a bit tentative at first, testing the waters, asking questions, listening, finding out what we have in common—in other words, getting acquainted.

In the interfaith dialogue, the process is much the same, although the social rituals that we might ordinarily rely on may need some modifications. In the interfaith dialogue, we're getting acquainted not just with a person but also with their beliefs, with their religion, with their faith traditions, which we may perceive as being quite different from ours, even perhaps threatening to ours.

In stage 1 of interfaith dialogue, our stories move us beyond separation and suspicion. Sharing our stories is often the first and best way to begin breaking down the barriers and building bridges. When we start talking about our families, how we grew up, where we lived, what our experiences have been, we can start to see each other not as the one who goes to synagogue on Saturdays, or who prays five times a day, or who takes communion every Sunday, but as another human being who has the same emotions and concerns that we do. Telling our stories begins to soften the hard boundaries that we think divide us, and it is a fundamental foundation for interfaith conversation and relationships.

Muriel Rukeyser, a twentieth-century American poet, once wrote, "The Universe is made of stories, not of atoms." This reminds us that not only do we shape our stories, but we are also shaped by our stories. Many of our stories were given to us by our parents and other important adults. You probably have stories about yourself that you don't remember personally, but you have heard them so often, they have become your own. When we share our stories, we have precious opportunities to understand their deeper nature and to expand them in positive directions. Each time we tell our stories, we not only meet each other, but we meet ourselves. So we share our stories in the hope that we might understand the uniqueness each of us brings to the relationship.

For the three of us—Pastor Don, Rabbi Ted, and Sheikh Jamal—our story is about interfaith from the inside out. When we first began working together after 9/11, we did not know exactly what the path before us would hold, but we believed that it would lead toward healing—not without difficulty, but toward healing nonetheless. Now our friendship goes way beyond tolerance and embraces a deep commitment to listening carefully and to honoring the experiences of the other. We have been able to confront the reality of the wounds for which each of our traditions has been or is responsible. As you can imagine, this did not happen immediately, and everywhere we speak or do workshops or give interviews, people want to know our stories, our background, and how our unlikely trio got together.

Recently, we had a dinner meeting at the Blue Star Cafe in Seattle. Ted was, as usual, wearing his *kippah,* the skullcap worn by many observing Jews, and Jamal had on his signature collarless shirt that gives him a vaguely clerical look. Don wasn't wearing a clergy collar, but there must have been something pastoral about his manner, for when the server came to our table she did a double take and asked who we were. After we told her, she said, "So am I really seeing the beginning of a story that starts with, 'A pastor, a rabbi, and a sheikh walk into a bar … '?"

So we'll start with that story—not of walking into a bar, but of how we came to interfaith, and to our congregations in Seattle. Not only is it the best way to introduce the context of our journey to you, but it offers an example of the kind of faith stories we have found it important to share, so we can move beyond the separations.

Each of us, each of you, comes to this interfaith journey out of particular life circumstances, beliefs, and history. As we share our unfolding stories with you, we hope our experiences will help you consider your own faith story as well as awaken your curiosity about the faith stories of people of other religions.

Pastor Don's Journey to Interfaith

On the surface, unless you notice that I am left-handed, I am a person of extreme privilege—white, male, straight, Protestant, educated. As a child, my dad's role as a college educator and my mother's role as a musician and teacher gave our family, it seemed to me, a privileged place in our community. As an adult, I went on to serve on the staff at Princeton Theological Seminary, and then three congregations all on or near college campuses. When I look back on my life, I sometimes wonder how I got to interfaith from such privilege.

There is a picture in my memory that helps me focus on the answer. It is a fall afternoon on a Saturday in Carlinville, a small college town on the plains of Illinois where the land looking north from town is as flat as a tabletop. The late afternoon rays of the sun shine almost parallel to the ground, turning the green leaves to gold. Church bells are ringing, and I can hear mourning doves. The air is pleasantly and comfortably warm with a slight breeze. A boy riding a sturdy Schwinn bike with a big basket is tossing copies of the *St. Louis Post-Dispatch* onto lawns on either side of my street, College Avenue. Our old black dog chases him halfheartedly. Life is calming down from the busy week now closing, and my family is about to gather for supper. The next day will begin the Christian Sabbath, the first day of the week, the day of resurrection, the day for church and rest and relaxation.

The year is sometime in the late 1940s. Even though we live only a block away from the college, there are woods across the street where we have forts and fantasies about being cowboys or explorers. I can be out of town in five minutes on my bike, riding past farms on gravel roads. My dad is dean of Blackburn College, my mother teaches piano, and our family is well-respected in this town. We are not wealthy, but thinking back now to that life, we had everything we needed. Life was good.

I realize now that, from the very beginning, my life was framed with blessings. My parents were skilled at helping my brother and me understand this. I did understand it, as much as that is possible for a child. Perhaps that is why the events I am about to describe made such an impression on me and penetrated my awareness with the reality of suffering in life.

Christmas of 1949 had us gathered in Leavenworth, Kansas, with my mother's family. Her sister and brother-in-law were visiting from Germany, where they were living after the war. My uncle Bill was in the army, and they had brought with them photographs of a bombed-out Germany and stories about Hitler and the Holocaust. Though I was only five years old, I realized, perhaps for the first time, that the world was not uniformly the way I had experienced it. I remember a feeling of crashing in slow motion, so slow I could stand almost outside myself and watch a part of what I had understood to be life coming apart. What remained was a simple sadness, an ache. How could such incredible suffering happen?

It was a defining moment for an unfolding of new and difficult realities. I have since learned that there were Jews living in Carlinville, but for the most part they did not identify themselves as such. There was no place for them to worship, no way for them to explain to me (without giving themselves away) that *Sabbath* is a reference to the seventh day of rest—not to Sunday, the first day of the week. They lived lives partly in secret. The stories that my aunt and uncle brought back from Germany gave me an understanding of why they might have done that.

About the same time, a minister in Kingston, Jamaica, wrote to my dad saying that he was sending two women to be students at Blackburn College. They were the first people of color to attend the college and to live in Carlinville. Gloria and Pearlie quickly worked their way into the fabric of life at Blackburn and became important members of the community. At Thanksgiving, the college did not recess; instead, there was a community Thanksgiving meal in the college dining room with faculty as hosts for each table of students. Most of the students waiting on the tables brought out trays with turkeys. Pearlie had hers balanced on her head—a vision of nobility and grace in the person of one excluded in those days from most halls of privilege. Again, it was a defining and transforming moment for me as a young boy. I think now the reason I remember this scene so clearly is that it started to replace what had crashed for me with the news about the Holocaust. With this scene I could feel hope replacing pain.

Looking back now, I would say that many of the choices I have made since then have been informed by the ways those two experiences impacted my life and showed me a vocation. The pleasant sound of the mourning doves had shifted to the sound of anguish for a brutal world, but one that also had the potential for genuine beauty and cooperation.

My years at Macalester College in St. Paul, Minnesota, took me more deeply into the larger issues of exclusion and inclusion.

Through a college program, I got a summer job at the Nile Hilton Hotel in Cairo, an experience that sparked my interest in the Middle East. When Judy and I decided to get married, we applied for teaching jobs at Gerard Institute in Sidon, Lebanon, an hour south of Beirut. We were both hired, and after graduation and our wedding, we bought a car in London and drove to Lebanon, taking ferries across the English Channel and the Bosphorus. The closer we got to Lebanon, the more I began to feel a sense of vocation, even though I did not know what was to come after our time in Sidon. At Gerard, many of my students were Palestinians from the refugee camp next to the school. They taught me something about being displaced, a teaching I took in. It continues to live within me, alongside the horrors of the Holocaust that I first learned about from my uncle Bill.

When the Six-Day War began on June 5, 1967, we were evacuated along with most of the other Americans living in the Middle East. We took a taxi from Sidon to the evacuation center at the American University in Beirut. We were shot at twice, probably because in the heat of that moment, many took Americans to be Israeli sympathizers, if not spies. I was sympathetic to both sides, but the danger we were in made it difficult to focus on anything other than our safety. Judy and I were sure we would be killed. Suddenly being confronted by the real possibility of one's own death puts everything on hold, including breathing. I had to remember to breathe and to take deep breaths to keep from getting dizzy. Neither of us could eat for several days, even after we had been evacuated to the safety of Ankara, Turkey. Sudden feelings of being unsteady kept coming back for about a year after we left Lebanon. My memory of the airport in Beirut as we were taking off reminds me of incomplete circles in my life.

We left many friends in Lebanon, and I thought we would return, but we did not. We eventually found our way back to New York, and I applied to the seminary at Princeton and began taking classes that summer, still hoping we might be able to go back. I even had dreams that we were in Sidon and everything was all right. That time in Lebanon was extremely important for me. My interfaith work is, in part, a way to complete that circle, and Judy and I hope someday to return to witness the reality of that place and what has happened since we left.

During the sixteen years we lived in Princeton, I completed seminary, worked there, and earned a PhD at New York University. In 1983, we moved to Hanover, New Hampshire, where the rabbi at Dartmouth, Daniel Siegel, and I became friends. Daniel reached out to me when I was the pastor at the Church of Christ at Dartmouth College, and it was from Daniel that I first began to learn about Jewish spirituality and to realize that, at heart, it is similar to Christian spirituality.

But the other blessing in Hanover was that Judy became the director of the International Office at Dartmouth. In addition to getting to know many students from all over the world, I developed a sense of the promises of diversity. Observing students explore similarities and differences with other students—and seeing the energy of their interest—taught me that diversity requires more than tolerance; differences can truly be a source of vitality, of beauty, and of strength.

While my vocation has centered on ministry, much of my passion for interfaith comes from another direction—music. My dad enjoyed music and my mother is a musician, a pianist still at ninety-seven. She taught me enough piano for me to develop a real passion for playing music. I learned percussion for the school band, and my parents bought me a guitar when I was fifteen. When I was seventeen, I worked at a YMCA Camp in the Ozarks, and it was there that I really learned to play the guitar and lead singing in the dining hall. The sound of exuberant campers singing together, unselfconsciously, is a sound of healing for me. That sounds says, "We can overcome our sorrows, we can help each other, and we can create a better world." Since then I have sung in several bands, and in 1979, helped form a band called "Life's Other Side," named for a song made famous by Hank Williams. We have been singing together now almost thirty years. (In 2005 we had the honor of singing at the Ernest Tubb Midnight Jamboree at the Grand Ole Opry!) It is the music, but even more than that, it is the experience of singing *together* that brings forth that passion for oneness made real in singing, and provides a strong part of the foundation for my role in the ministry that I share with Jamal and Ted.

Rabbi Ted's Journey to Interfaith

My first encounters with "interfaith" were filled with pain.

It never occurred to me that I grew up in a Jewish area of Cleveland Heights until we moved to a new suburban community where we were the only Jews on the street, and I was among just three Jews in the high school. Not only was I "the new kid" when I entered the ninth grade there, I was different.

"Hey," the class bully challenged me that first day in the boys' room, "are you a Jew?"

"Yes," I answered, and felt his fist punch all the breath out of me. I remember stumbling out of the washroom, trying not to cry. As the weeks went by, I did make some friends, but even they were intimidated by those boys who took delight in calling me names. Perhaps that's what hurt me the most—that even my friends were silent in the face of the threats and the name-calling. Halfway through that year, my best friend, a Catholic, told me that he could no longer come to my house after school. His parents had found out that I was Jewish, and they didn't want him going to a Jewish home.

Our new next-door neighbors were a Catholic family. Upon learning that we were Jewish, they had a fence built with its ugly infrastructure exposed on our side. I remember my father going to City Hall to complain, and I remember the fence coming down. Our neighbors on that side still didn't talk to us, but at least the yard felt open again.

I was born a month after the attack on Pearl Harbor and grew up in the shadow of the Holocaust, but I never understood the paranoia I sensed in my parents until my adventures in the ninth grade and in that first year in our new house. Although I switched to a different school beginning in the tenth grade, something had happened that changed me. Whenever possible, I did not offer the information that I was Jewish. I just wished I could fit in.

Fitting in, however, was not easy. Even in my own extended family there were difficulties. We were Reform Jews, and I attended religious school on Sundays as well as Hebrew school one or two afternoons a week. We welcomed Shabbat every Friday dinner, sharing blessings over Sabbath candles, wine, and the special sweet bread called challah. We observed the holidays through the year, but when we visited my father's family, it was clear that they did not consider us "properly" Jewish. My paternal grandfather belittled the lack of a Yiddish accent in the Hebrew that my sister and I were learning to read. We were not doing it right. I felt that I was getting it from both sides, and religion was clearly not a safe thing. My Jewish identity could draw violence from non-Jews and harsh criticism from Jews.

I did my undergraduate work at Ohio University in Athens, Ohio, certainly not a Jewish environment in those days. In the freshman dorm, I found my Jewishness something of a curiosity to many of my classmates, and I got points for bringing the rather exotic (at the time) bag of bagels back from home. Although I wasn't attacked, I was clearly different. The only way to get out of the dorm was to join a fraternity, and in those days, there were only two fraternities on campus that accepted Jewish students. One was all-Jewish, and the other was the campus "Animal House." As a self-described misfit, I fit there and coexisted easily with others whether they were Jewish or not.

My early interfaith adventures consisted of asking questions of Christian friends: "If Jesus came to die for your sins, didn't he *have* to die? And if he had to die, why blame those who helped that happen? Why would Christians hate the Jews for being 'Christ killers' if they were simply—to the extent they had any real power at that time—enabling the end that was necessary? And why would Judas be the evil one if he was carrying out what was required?"

I never got much of an answer to these questions, but even being able to ask them was freeing for me. Then in my senior year of college, I discovered the writings of Martin Buber, and I found in his teachings profound relevance for my life. I chose to enter rabbinical school because I believed that would provide a foundation for me to study and teach about Martin Buber and the difference between what he described as an *I-It* and an *I-Thou* relationship. What I discovered, to my dismay, was that Martin Buber was not a favorite of professors at the rabbinical seminary. He was not practicing his Jewishness in a way they would have liked, and he identified with none of the Jewish religious movements. And, from the beginning, although an early citizen of Israel, he was in favor of a binational state, a point of view not supported by the mainstream Jewish community.

The first folks I found with whom I could talk freely about Buber were not Jewish. To them, Buber was clearly a Jew, but they were upset neither by his lack of observance nor by his early belief in a binational State of Israel. I began to see that Buber, although teaching from Jewish sources, was teaching a kind of universalism based on eighteenth-century Hasidic teachers, but leading beyond all particular teachers and teachings.

In Los Angeles, as an assistant rabbi in 1968, I was introduced to a Benedictine priory, a small community of men in the upper desert several hours north of the city, where we held retreats. Even after I left my congregational position, I continued to bring groups to St. Andrew's Priory over the twenty-five years I was in Los Angeles. In precious and lengthy conversations with some of the monks, I began to heal old wounds. We prayed together. We talked about our similarities and our differences. There was a mutuality of respect that felt natural and good. It was clear to me that our different paths led to a shared Universal.

Although Martin Buber remained a central teacher for me, I realize now that I went through a period when my major teachers were not Jewish. Through meditative practices that were, at first, Hindu and Zen Buddhist, I learned about expanded states of awareness from the inside out. Only after this introduction did I discover teachings in meditation from the Jewish tradition.

I learned from Ram Dass, a Jewish professor of psychology turned Hindu, and from Alan Watts, an Episcopal priest who left that calling in order to teach psychology and spirituality. The writings of a Newport Beach, California, preacher named Neville Goddard surprised me with instructions on how to look at my own Torah from a metaphysical point of view. The books of Joel Goldsmith, a teacher of his own path called the Infinite Way, taught me of other depths of spirituality that flowed from scripture.

These non-Jewish teachers and teachings allowed me to discover depths within my own tradition to which I had been blind before. It was clear that spirituality was a universal pursuit, and the value of any particular path was the degree to which it supported the journey toward that universal awareness.

In Seattle, to which we moved in 1993, far more extensive interfaith opportunities became available for me. Perhaps it was the Pacific Northwest, perhaps it was the times, perhaps it was both, but remarkable opportunities for interfaith spiritual dialogue presented themselves, and within them I felt a deep experience of authenticity. I was clearly "Rabbi," and I was clearly "Jewish," but I was able to celebrate my calling and my tradition as foundations for a universal quest. It became apparent to me that each authentic spiritual tradition has special gifts to bring, gifts that can help us all in our journey.

Once I realized the reality of Oneness—not simply as a concept but as a Truth of Being—I had to honor the authenticity of all paths toward that One. Although deeply rooted in my own Jewish identity and tradition, I continually seek to celebrate the treasures in all faith paths. And when any faith, by announcing itself to be the "only way" to God, inhibits this celebration, I understand that faith to be essentially diminishing the very God to whom its adherents pray. We are in this life together, and our greater happiness comes when we are able to support each other in meaningful ways.

Sheikh Jamal's Journey to Interfaith

My journey to interfaith is rooted in my family's teachings and insights. From my father I learned the beauty of studying other religions and cultures, and from my mother I learned that interfaith is about the essential work of creating inner spaciousness by opening the heart. My beloved parents often spoke about interfaith not as conversion but as completion—becoming a more complete human being—and their words resonated in my heart. The only time I discerned some pain and bewilderment in my parents about the topic of interfaith was when they talked about their personal suffering during the horrific rioting and killing between Muslims and Hindus in 1947, during the partition of India and Pakistan. But this served to deepen my interest in working in a vocation that promoted understanding and peace between religions.

My father was a professional diplomat representing Pakistan, and after the country separated into two nation-states in 1971, he represented the State of Bangladesh. A devoted Muslim who was deeply versed in Islam, he enjoyed learning about other faiths and often remarked that this knowledge broadened and deepened his understanding of verses in the Qur'an. In the non-Muslim countries my father was assigned to, my parents happily allowed their children to accompany friends to churches and Hindu and Buddhist temples, and to participate in Jewish festivals. My father delighted in reminding those around him that the second-most used word in the Qur'an after *Allah* is *ilm*, meaning "knowledge." Indeed, a prayer in the Qur'an pleads, "O God, advance me in knowledge" (20:114) and the Prophet Muhammad said, "Seek knowledge from cradle to grave." Father lamented the fact that, ever since the precipitous decline of the economic and political base of the Islamic countries in the last three hundred years, the majority of Muslims have been reduced to the poorest and most illiterate bloc in the world.

My father acquired his spacious outlook from his parents. His mother was a gentle soul who worked tirelessly for the rights of women in the conservative environment of her village, and through her example he, too, became a women's rights advocate. His father was a highly respected teacher and healer with an awe-inspiring education in Islam and spiritual healing. For over a dozen years he studied in Deoband in northern India, a renowned religious and academic center in the Islamic world. My paternal grandparents were Sufis, but they did not always identify themselves as such because that might be considered boastful. One aspires to be a Sufi in one's heart, and it seems pretentious to talk about such a private relationship in public. Sufis—either Sunni or Shia, the two major denominations of Islam—are dedicated more to living the spirit of Islam than to dotting the *i*'s and crossing the *t*'s of Islamic law. Sufis do follow the rituals and prescriptions of Islam, but are focused more on essence than on form, on compassion and awareness rather than on strict adherence to religious practice. My grandparents walked the Sufi path and made sure that their children were rooted in Sufi spirituality, as well as the fundamental tenets of Islam.

My grandfather, though sought-after by prestigious colleges in Calcutta, refused to teach there because he was deeply opposed to British rule. Determined to fight colonial rule by "noncooperation" with the occupying government, he committed his life instead to serving his village as a scholar and teacher of Islam, Arabic, and Persian, and as a spiritual healer. To his intimates and students he spoke constantly of the need to cultivate inner spaciousness. Thus *spaciousness* became a familiar word in our household, and it is not surprising that one of my favorite verses in the Qur'an says, "Allah has made the earth for you as a carpet spread out that you may go about therein on spacious roads" (71:18–19).

My mother grew up in a small town not far from my father's village. Compassionate by nature and fiercely devoted to the betterment of daily life for the women of her culture, she was deeply resentful of clerics and institutions, whom she blamed for not granting women their rights so fully enshrined in the Qur'an and in the sayings (*Hadith*) and conduct (*Sunnah*) of the Prophet. She also blamed the clerics for inciting religious riots between Muslims and Hindus. Much of her wisdom she probably acquired from her own mother, a deeply spiritual and devout Muslim, who placed her faith more in God than in the clerics of her village. When my mother's father, a prominent lawyer and activist, died at a young age, her mother defied the urgings of the patriarchal clerics and the men in her family and refused to remarry or turn over her earthly affairs to a male relative. Instead, she single-handedly raised six children and miraculously was able to send four of them to graduate schools in the United States and England.

Both my mother and her mother eagerly pointed out that there is no official priesthood or religious ordination in Islam, that the relationship between humanity and God is direct. They freely quoted the Prophet Muhammad's famous saying, "Every Muslim is his own priest." My mother's favorite joke was the teaching story of the timeless Mulla Nasruddin. When he was asked why it is that clerics always sport a pointed beard, the mulla replied, "Simple. The clerics are always falling on their faces, and the easiest way to pick them up is by their beards!"

My mother's message was clear: Harmony between religions is not possible without doing the inner work that creates the spaciousness required to embrace differences. A slavish attachment to and reliance on clerics and religious institutions is an easy way to avoid doing the inconvenient but real work so clearly outlined in the Qur'an: "God does not change [people's] condition unless they change their inner selves" (13:11, trans. Asad).

My understanding of interfaith deepened when my parents were posted to Iran and Turkey. There I delighted in studying the works of the famous thirteenth-century Islamic theologian and poet Jalaluddin Rumi. To many Muslims, Rumi is a second Muhammad, and the collection of his utterances, a second Qur'an. In Iran and Turkey, I experienced the joy of studying the Qur'an in tandem with verses of Rumi. Basing his teachings on meditations about the inner meanings of the Qur'an, the sage pleads with us fervently to open up our hearts so that we can become fully human and evolve into a higher awareness. "To God belong the most beautiful names" (59:24) and "Our God and your God is One" (29:46) proclaims the Qur'an. Rumi compares the religions of the world to branches of a tree: swaying differently in the breeze, they are all connected at the roots.

It often comes as a surprise to non-Muslims in the West that Islam honors religious diversity, but in fact the Qur'an contains a number of verses that espouse inclusivity and celebrate diversity. If God wanted, says the Qur'an, God could have made all of humanity one single community, but out of compassion God chose diversity so that we might "vie, then, with one another in doing good works!" (5:48, trans. Asad) and so that we might "get to know one another" (49:13).

Given that my parents carried deep wounds from the religious massacres during the 1947 partition of the Indian subcontinent, their spacious modeling of these verses in their own lives is remarkable. As Hindus from Pakistan migrated to India and Muslims from India fled to Pakistan, over a million people were brutally killed in the frenzy of political and religious passions. Over the years my parents talked about the personal traumas they suffered during the partition. As a child, I empathized with their anguish as they recalled the death of a beloved relative at the hands of Hindu fanatics, and I remember feeling a visceral hatred for and terror toward Hindus. But my parents were quick to point out that Hindus also were killed by Muslim extremists, and they told many stories of Hindus heroically harboring their Muslim neighbors and friends. These true stories of compassion, courage, and heroic actions by both Hindus and Muslims in this crazed time touched me and my siblings profoundly, and we often asked our parents to tell us more about the true-life bravery and love they had witnessed during that tragic chapter of south Asian history.

I now realize that, as our parents shared their pain openly with us, they were embracing their suffering and gently healing their wounds. When they recounted situations of love and bravery by Muslims and Hindus in extraordinarily trying times, encouraged their children to visit Hindu temples, and greeted their Hindu friends with true warmth and sincerity, they not only softened their pain but transformed it into a blessing. That blessing endures into the next generation. For this gift, my siblings and I are deeply grateful to our beloved parents.

As I approached adulthood, though I was fully immersed in the Islamic world and Sufi spirituality, there was an expectation that I receive a Western degree that would afford me a conventional profession and a conventional life. My studies took me first to England to study law at Lincoln's Inn. Although I enjoyed my studies, my two years in London were marred by frequent run-ins with hate groups called *skinheads*. Hearing myself called derogatory names such as "Paki" and "WOG" ("Western Oriental Gentlemen") did not bother me at first, but I soon began to feel self-conscious about my skin color and nationality as I never had before. In a palpable way, I realized that my skin color was a problem.

One night my anxiety turned to fear when a group of skinheads began to attack me in an underground tube station. Yelling the usual epithets, they let loose with a furious volley of stones in my direction. Luckily, their aim was lousy and I was a fast runner. But I was scarred by the incident. I felt unsafe and wary of being alone in the streets, especially at night. I sought refuge by transferring, with the help of my parents, to the United States, where, during my two years at the University of Oregon in Eugene, I especially enjoyed working with the community of a large and diverse foreign student body. It was refreshing to find that my skin color, nationality, and religion were sources of exotic interest to the people I met as a foreign student in 1970s America. My sense of self was restored and my fear subsided. I became immersed in student activism and was elected president of the Foreign Student Organization, an experience that taught me the value of collaborating with campus and state organizations. We lobbied to lower tuition for foreign students, raised funds for cyclone survivors in what was then East Pakistan, and worked to heighten awareness about the role of the U.S. government in supporting authoritarian regimes in developing countries. I enjoyed the taste of success, but at the same time I experienced a gnawing dissatisfaction with the study of economics and the direction that was leading me in.

In the fall of 1972, I started graduate studies at the University of California at Berkeley. Daily, as I walked the famous street called Telegraph Avenue to get to campus, I savored the aromas of the ethnic cuisines wafting from the exotic eateries. The aromas stimulated an intense hunger, but I soon realized that my hunger was not actually for food; I was hungering to study spirituality. Soon after receiving my master's degree in political science, I felt a call to move in the direction of the ministry that is so dear to my heart today, and I returned home to study Islamic spirituality under the tutelage of my revered parents.

Six years later, I came back to the United States and settled in Seattle to seek a way to define and live out my ministry. Some years later, the sudden and tragic deaths of both my parents within days of each other swept aside any remaining uncertainties I had about my life's purpose. I woke up to the words of the Prophet Muhammad: "Move from knowledge of the tongue to knowledge of the heart." More than ever, I realized that what really sustained my love for interfaith was my parents' modeling of the Qur'anic verses about diversity and inclusiveness.

How We Got Together

Although our individual paths had prepared us for coming together in a deep interfaith friendship, our story together didn't actually start until Pastor Don and Rabbi Ted met in 1999 at a monthly meeting for Christian-Jewish dialogue in Seattle. At one point, they were assigned to make a joint presentation on a book the group was studying. There ensued a number of phone and lunch conversations, during which they discovered how much they shared in terms of their concerns for the world, the practice of ministry, and their hopes for the future.

At the time, Don was serving as minister and head of staff at University Congregational United Church of Christ, which has a history of interest in and support for interfaith activities dating back to the 1960s. The year before he met Ted, Don had been chairing the Palestinian Concerns Task Force of the Church Council of Greater Seattle and had been invited to be a part of a steering committee helping to organize a Holocaust scholars' conference at the University of Washington. During one of those meetings, Don recalls, "I heard a member of the group describe some of the history of anti-Semitism, and I realized that I needed to learn more about that history, especially as a Christian pastor and religious leader. At a friend's recommendation, I read *The Crucifixion of the Jews: The Failure of Christians to Understand the Jewish Experience*, by Franklin H. Littell.

"I discovered, with growing horror, the degree to which the Christian church had given theological assent to the Holocaust. Centuries of anti-Judaism had culminated in the murder of millions of Jews. I was weak in the knees, and even wondered if I could go on as a minister of a Christian church. I wondered how I could be a minister and not have fully understood this. How could it be that Christianity, representing the Gospel of Jesus, would give support to such suffering?" It was soon after this experience that Pastor Don joined the Jewish-Christian Dialogue at Roanoke House in Seattle, where he met Rabbi Ted.

Prior to arriving in Seattle, Ted had started out on his journey to become a rabbi in the traditional ways: rabbinical school, five-and-a-half years at Hebrew Union College–Jewish Institute of

Religion in Cincinnati. Yet he never felt that he fit in as a rabbi. After exploring the worlds of the Human Potential Movement in the late sixties, he began doing intense small-group work with his congregation, but he was increasingly aware of his discomfort performing the duties of a "regular" rabbi.

At one point, after reading the text of a Shabbat service, Ted realized, "The words simply were not true for me. The work I was doing did not support a spiritual vision of inclusivity. Instead, it supported only the continuity of the separate culture of Judaism. Where my rabbinic colleagues sought to preserve Judaism, I was seeking the teachings in Judaism that supported a greater spiritual journey."

Ted began working on a doctorate in clinical psychology and left his position as a Hillel rabbi. Yet, to his surprise, he discovered a very different way of being a rabbi: "I found myself called to an entirely different kind of ministry. For the first time, I felt that I was 'Rabbi.' It had nothing to do with a job. It had to do with an identity." After graduating from the California School for Professional Psychology in 1975 and going into private practice, Ted began to teach a psychospiritual approach to Torah, finding the ancient text opening in profound ways, not only as an outer story, but as an inner story relating to his spiritual quest.

By the time Ted and his wife, Ruth Neuwald Falcon, arrived in Seattle, they were ready to create the synagogue community in Seattle called Bet Alef Meditative Synagogue. *Alef* and *bet* are the first two letters of the Hebrew alphabet. *Alef* is a silent letter with which the alphabet begins, as if to say, "All speech begins with silence." *Bet* is a word that means "house," so *bet alef* means "a house for spirit." The Bet Alef Meditative Synagogue became a meditative community unique in the Seattle area, and it was out of Ted's blend of private practice in counseling and the Bet Alef community that he came to meet Don.

One of the first things they discovered was that they made each other laugh. It wasn't in telling jokes, but more in the way they looked at life. Ted would say things that were clearly exaggerations, and it always took Don a minute or two to realize what was going on, prompting Don to say, "But seriously, folks!"

About the same time, Rabbi Ted happened to meet Sheikh Jamal through participation on a board that was developing a graduate-level university focusing on spiritual studies. The university never got off the ground, but those meetings provided the foundation for a deep friendship. Jamal became Ted's sheikh, and Ted became Jamal's rabbi.

Jamal had settled in Seattle to seek a way to live out his ministry after the sudden and tragic death of his parents. He had begun teaching classes at home on inner transformation, and a lasting community of fellow seekers who ate, played, and prayed together emerged. Inspired by Rumi's verse, "Come out of the circle of time and enter the circle of love," they called themselves "Circle of Love."

Much to Jamal's surprise, a steady number of people came to these classes, and the numbers grew exponentially, as did their program of Sunday services, meditation classes, spiritual psychology classes, and retreats. Even though a couple of members had very large homes in which they could meet, when the Circle increased to three hundred, they evolved into the Interfaith Community Church. Many Christians in the community—and they constitute the majority—asked out of graciousness that the word *church* be replaced by a more inclusive term. Some of the Muslims, equally graciously, insisted that the name *church*, which means "gathering place," remain. They agreed to follow the wisdom of the Prophet Muhammad, who, when visited in the seventh century by delegations of Christians and Jews, asked that they conduct Sunday services and Shabbat worship in the mosque, for "it is simply a place consecrated to God."

When Jamal describes his congregation today, he rejoices in this group of people from a variety of religious backgrounds—some rooted in their own traditions, who water those roots by being open to the insights and practices of others; some creating their own personal path by exploring different teachings and practices of the world's religions. "By the grace of God, we have created a harmonious framework for differences to be brought into the open and received with respect, compassion, and a collective resolve to find creative solutions. We are committed to the sacred task of fostering a living, breathing, harmonious interfaith community."

Each of us—Don, Ted, and Jamal—had come to this particular point in time through wide-ranging and circuitous paths, and each had come from a rich tradition of faith and commitment to interfaith. Yet it wasn't until after the events of 9/11 that things began to come together for us in a significant way.

On the Friday evening following that explosive Tuesday, Ted organized an interfaith worship experience for the Shabbat and invited Jamal to co-lead. An overflow crowd showed up to join in grieving the loss of lives and the loss of innocence. For the first time in our memory, our own country had been attacked. With teachings from Jewish and Islamic sources, we shared meditations honoring our grief and inviting compassion. We began together to dream of the greater healing that could emerge from the violence of that week. Jamal's presence allowed Ted's synagogue community to know a more peaceful face of Islam, and a deep friendship was born.

Jamal and Ted continued to work together, both at prayer services and through classes, to make available to a non-Muslim audience the deep spiritual resources of Islam. When more Muslims became involved, communities began speaking to each other on matters of substance. They called their expanding organization Unity Project Seattle and began to connect with other faith communities. The organization has since become the Northwest Interfaith Community Outreach and is now run by lay leaders.

When the first anniversary of 9/11 approached, Ted and Jamal began working on an interfaith day of study, conversation, and worship. Given Ted's connection with Don in the Jewish-Christian Dialogue group, it was a natural for Ted to give Don a call, inviting him to participate. When Ted mentioned that Jamal would be involved, Don's response was, "I've seen Jamal's picture in *Yes!* magazine [a progressive and hopeful publication printed in the Northwest], and I believe any friend of *Yes!* will be a friend of mine."

It was almost as if decades of three long journeys coalesced within this one phrase: *A friend of mine.*

Pastor Don's agreement to join Rabbi Ted and Sheikh Jamal signaled the first step of what would develop into lifelong friendship that would have a significant impact on all three of us, in our personal lives, in our individual faiths, and in our interfaith ministries.

Forging a Path

We believe we offer a living message that it is possible to move beyond the separations and suspicions that could divide us by listening to each other's stories and genuinely getting to know each other. We began as concerned colleagues and religious leaders of congregations in Seattle. Along the way, we discovered ourselves in a friendship far beyond simple tolerance; we came to share appreciation and thanksgiving for our differences as well as for our similarities. We do not seek to minimize our differences, but to learn from them. Together, we seek to discover and to celebrate the life that we share. We have some appreciation that we are each forging a path toward deepening community. As we do, we are discovering that our roots in our own traditions deepen. We are each more committed than ever to our own path, perhaps because we are able, through the lens of another's tradition, to appreciate hidden depths within our own faith.

We invite you to engage with us in an expansive spiritual journey. Each of you reading this book has your own version of interfaith experiences, maybe from things that happened long before the word *interfaith* became a conscious thought. As you consider this first stage of getting to the heart of interfaith, you might want to reflect on your own faith background and the early stories you remember about your family's religious teachings. How did your family view people of different faiths, and how does that affect your views today? What life experiences have influenced your interest in other faiths? If you are at this beginning stage of interfaith dialogue, we can't emphasize enough the importance of being intentional about getting acquainted. Take some steps to put yourself in a situation where you have an opportunity to get to know someone of another faith. Ask them about their faith experiences. Explore together how you got to this point of being interested in interfaith dialogue.

This point of personal connection is where it all begins.

∞

3

THE CORE OF OUR TRADITIONS

Inquiring More Deeply

Timeless Teachings

When we are getting acquainted with someone new, we are constantly sifting our first impressions, sorting what we want to say, wondering how the other person is responding to us. As we begin to learn more about people, what their stories are, what their life experiences have been, we naturally shift to a deeper level of conversation. We start to find out what is important to them.

In an interfaith context, we are moving into stage 2, inquiring more deeply. We might be curious about people's worship rituals; we might want to know more about their spiritual practices. But, most important, this is a time of getting to know what their core beliefs are.

When we move beneath the surface to learn about the foundation of another's faith, we can better appreciate the more observable aspects of that tradition. We are also more likely to glimpse the timeless teachings contained in each faith we examine that speak of universals to which we can all relate more fully.

Moving into the deeper inquiry of stage 2 is not without its hazards. It's very easy to hear someone else's beliefs with a comparative, even judgmental, mind-set: How does this differ from what I believe? Is it "right" or "wrong"? Which religion is "better"? This kind of evaluative listening throws up huge roadblocks to interfaith dialogue and collaboration. We might wonder if it is really okay to find true meaning in another faith. Are we in danger of forfeiting our own beliefs?

We believe that each of our faith identities can be enriched through the treasures of other faiths. The goal of deeper inquiry in stage 2 is not to determine "who wins the religion contest," but to develop a truly appreciative understanding of each other's faith.

Deeper inquiry also calls for a kind of listening different from that in stage 1. Stage 2 takes us beyond suspicion into listening that opens us to the essence, the beauty, the truth of someone else's core beliefs. This level of inquiry requires a relational foundation that communicates, "I want to hear; I want to know more." It requires a certain amount of shared experience. We need to know enough about the other person so that we can entrust them with what matters most to us. We need to know that they will listen to us and not try to change our minds about our own commitments of faith. We need a comfortable context for sharing.

By the time the three of us got to this stage, we were jokingly calling ourselves the interfaith "Rat Pack," after a mid-1950s and 1960s group of entertainers that included Dean Martin, Sammy Davis Jr., and Joey Bishop. We knew a bit about each other's idiosyncrasies. Pastor Don was the musician among us who was already primed to use music in the service of spiritual teaching. Sheikh Jamal could dance to the poetry of Rumi, and his energy was always welcoming. And Rabbi Ted, well, Ted could find humor when we least expected it. (Actually, the word *humor* is hardly adequate. Ted doesn't tell jokes; he delivers one-liners in the tradition of Groucho Marx or Milton Berle, two of the greatest comedians of the twentieth century.)

There are also ways in which any two of us share connections—a somewhat unusual, but very fortunate reality for us. Rabbi Ted and Sheikh Jamal, for example, share a tradition grounded in texts written in their original languages, and because Arabic and

Hebrew are related languages, there are often remarkable similarities for them to discover. Pastor Don and Sheikh Jamal, on the other hand, are both part of the majority in many countries and areas of the world: there are 1.7 billion Muslims, 2.1 billion Christians, and only 15 million Jews. And Rabbi Ted and Pastor Don share a common Western heritage. Although they often interpret the text differently, both Rabbinic Judaism and Christianity are based on shared biblical writings. In each case, this had enabled us to appreciate and to understand each other better. We are continually grateful for the myriad ways our friendship continues to grow.

In other words, we already had built a context for each of us to share the authenticity of our own traditions. Because of the mutual respect and affection we shared for each other, we were able to go more deeply into mutual discovery of each other's beliefs. We began to consider what might help us convey the essential teaching of our tradition.

We asked ourselves, "Is there a single verse, or a single story, that reflects the essential teaching of Judaism, of Christianity, and of Islam? What one verse, for example, would we take with us to a desert island?" We suspected that this opportunity would help each of us share the core of our traditions, and perhaps explain why each of our traditions is so important to us. It's always a little dangerous to pick "one teaching," or "one verse," but we learned a lot through this process. This chapter is the result of this exploration.

Pastor Don: Love

> This is my commandment, that you love one another as I
> have loved you.
> —John 15:12

I like this verse because it points so directly to the transformative possibilities of love and of faith. I like it because it describes so clearly what is necessary for us to cooperate with God's purposes, challenging the status quo and helping those in need. This verse describes the love that supports the oneness that brings healing to this world. And I like it because of the way it connects with Ted and Jamal. Yet, I almost didn't choose it as the essential Christian teaching I wanted to share with them.

For starters, I have always disliked the common Christian saying that the New Testament is about *love*, and the Old Testament is about *law*. This misunderstanding actually came about when the early Greek translation of the Hebrew word *Torah* (which means "teaching") as *nomos* was eventually translated into English as "law." While this is one of the meanings of *nomos*, it is not an accurate translation of *Torah*. *Love* appears in the Old Testament also, but the standard Christian sense has been that love supersedes law or legality, that it's *better* than legality and, therefore, Christianity supersedes Judaism. In other words, this use of the word *love* is a building block of anti-Semitism, of anti-Judaism.

So I intentionally avoided writing about love. I tried out some other options: the golden rule (important, but it appears in all of our traditions); the story of the Good Samaritan (about compassion: a *consequence* of love); and the parable of the Prodigal Son (about forgiveness, also a *consequence* of love). Nothing seemed quite right. Finally, Ted and Jamal and I had a serious conversation about this, and they convinced me that I needed to write about love. But I thought I at least needed to start with the problems related to this complex four-letter word.

THE WORD *LOVE* IS A PROBLEM. Twenty-five years ago when I read M. Scott Peck's book *The Road Less Traveled*, the first words jumped out at me: "Life is difficult." I could *feel* the power in those words because they were naming a truth that we do our best to ignore. We live in a world that wants to cover the reality of difficulty with advertising and hype that tell us that we can be whatever we want to be. That we deserve something better. That we can realize our desires if we just buy this or that. Then we will be the people we had dreamed of becoming!

This way of thinking contradicts the irrepressible reality that life really *is* difficult. We can buy all we want, but we can't buy happiness because we can't buy love. We can't buy love, but we can give it and receive it. We already have it. It is available, but we don't always use it or receive it. We have it, but we often don't know it. While love can help us cope with our difficulties, the problem is that we don't really practice it in the way Jesus commands. Love is the most powerful force in the universe, but we don't know what to do with it. The word *love* is a problem because we don't *get* it.

Look at the verse I quoted from John 15. It has a strong, solid beginning: "This is my commandment." The word *commandment* points to moral authority rooted in God and voiced by a prophet acting on God's behalf. So the statement moves us to take what follows very seriously. But what follows, well, is not so certain: "Love one another as I have loved you."

The word *love* is a problem because it has too many different meanings.

We use the word *love* in so many different ways: "I just love your new dress!" "I loved that book!" "I love you!" And when we go back to the original Greek to try to get some clarity, we run into another problem. The Greek word translated as *love* in this verse is *agape.* But there are two other words in Greek that also mean love. *Eros* is the love we talk about in "making love." *Philios* is the love we talk about when we love objects, ideas, friends, certain kinds of affiliations. There are connections to *agape,* but the meanings of *eros* and *philios* are related to our personal satisfaction, while *agape* points to something much broader and deeper.

WHAT IS LOVE? *Agape* has to do with the love of God, the love that God is, the relationship between God and Jesus, and the relationships that we have to each other and to God. In other words, it is not merely an affiliation, a simple connection, something pleasing.

Agape is like binding energy in an atom. If you take the separate parts of an atom and weigh them, and then weigh the atom as a whole, you will find that the atom weighs less than the sum of its parts. That's because some of the matter has been converted to energy to hold the pieces together—binding energy. (This is the only thing I remember from college chemistry, but it clearly made a big impression on me.)

But even more importantly, *agape* lifts us above the needs and concerns of the self to a different level of identity, to a different level of spiritual awareness. For example, certain types of love could fulfill our ordinary but powerful yearnings to be loved by someone, to find someone who would make us feel complete, fulfilled, worthy, honored, and respected. But the irony is that we can't get there by focusing on our own needs. The love that is *agape* comes to us through the opening of our hearts to the needs of others. As we find a new identity in that love, we also rise to a new level of spirituality because this love comes from, and is, God. We can't make it. We can't manipulate it. But it can create us, heal us, redeem us, forgive us.

BUT HOW DO WE *GET* IT? What I am suggesting is that *agape* love is similar to faith. They both frame the way we see life. But, still, we're left with the question: How do we *get* love? I think a clue to this lies in what Dietrich Bonhoeffer, the German pastor who was executed by the Nazis for his role in a plot to kill Hitler, had to say about faith:

> I discovered later, and I'm still discovering right up to this moment, that it is only by living completely in this world, that one learns to have faith. By this worldliness I mean living unreservedly in life's duties, problems, successes, and failures—in so doing we throw ourselves completely into the arms of God, taking seriously not our own sufferings, but those of God in the world. That, I think, is faith.
> —*Dietrich Bonhoeffer to Eberhard Bethge, July 21, 1944*

The line that leaps out at me is that we are to "throw ourselves completely into the arms of God." When we are trapped by ordinary selfish concerns, our identities are restricted to very narrow conditions—sadness, failure, emptiness, even pleasure and certain kinds of satisfactions. There is no ultimate satisfaction though, and we go to greater and greater extremes. And the further we go, the less satisfied we become. But when we are able to open our hearts, as Bonhoeffer suggests, and concern ourselves with the concerns of God, *our* concerns are met because we are then filled with love.

The meaning of the word *covenant* helps me to understand this. It is rooted in the experience of treaties from the ancient Near East that expressed the "shape of reality." It was a way of saying, "This is the way things are. This is the way we will 'see' life." I think the way we are to understand Jesus's use of love, of *agape*, is just that: Love provides a particular lens through which we see life.

In Miguel de Cervantes's novel *Don Quixote*, Don Quixote is in love with a woman named Aldonzo Lorenzo. She is a barmaid, but Don Quixote calls her his lovely Lady Dulcinea. She is a dominant figure in the shape of his reality, and he trusts that she is real—real in the way she exists in his imagination. He knows that this might not, in fact, be the same way others see her, but that does not matter to him. He chooses to act as if the world were what he would have it be. He sees Dulcinea through eyes of love.

I believe that, when we see through the eyes of love, we love one another as Jesus loved his disciples, and we are living the reality that God intends for us.

LOVE IN ACTION. Loving our neighbors as ourselves has been a part of Abrahamic monotheism since the time of the Exodus from Egypt when the book of Leviticus was originally conceived. "You shall love your neighbor as yourself" is found in the book of Leviticus, chapter 19, verse 18. So the concept of love was certainly not new with Jesus. What *was* new with Jesus were the ways he demonstrated love, the stories he told about love, the examples he gave us. There are five illustrations of *agape* love that are among my favorites. In all these stories, Jesus acts on an authority that he believes is divine and uses that authority *with love* to make real the love that God is.

Unconventional love. There is a story in each of the four Gospels about a woman who brings expensive ointment and rubs it on Jesus's feet (Luke 7:38; John 12:38) or head (Matthew 26:6; Mark 14:3). In three of the Gospels (Matthew, Mark, and John), Judas strongly objects because the ointment might have been sold and the money used to help the poor. But Jesus objects to the objection, insisting that what the woman has done will be told in memory of her. The fourth story in Luke carries the thread of compassion further. There, Jesus explains to the disciples that the care the woman has shown to him reflects God's concern for him. This is a story that suggests that how we love each other may often run counter to conventional wisdom.

Love without limits. The story of the Woman at the Well (John 4:1–26) is an extended story of Jesus's love for another human being, someone who eventually confesses her need for "living water." Jesus, a Jew, asks for a drink of water at a well from a woman who is a Samaritan. She is amazed because Jews ordinarily don't have anything to do with Samaritans. Jesus, however, not only treats her as a full and complete human being, but, as he does so, he also suggests that his spiritual teachings constitute what he calls "living water." He treats the woman with love because of his faith, because of the way he sees life. His treatment of her is life-giving to both of them.

Love in action. In the story of the Prodigal Son, the younger son decides that it is time to take his inheritance and strike out on his own. He travels to a distant country, wastes his money, and then realizes that he must find a job or he will die. He gets a job feeding pigs, but hates it. Finally, he decides to go home, hoping to work for his father. The surprise is that his father welcomes him home with open and loving arms and gives him a party. This is truly love in action.

Love and forgiveness. Peter, whom Jesus regarded as a beloved disciple, denied his association with Jesus (Matthew 26:69–75), and yet, later, Peter became the first head of the church. This is a story that leads to Jesus's forgiving of Peter, but, in the same way that the parent forgives the son in the story of the Prodigal Son, the consequence is not a return to ordinary life. Something extraordinary and entirely unexpected happens as a consequence of the forgiveness.

Love and neighbor. Jesus also tells a story about a man traveling from Jerusalem to Jericho who is attacked by robbers who beat him and leave him to die. Two religious leaders walk by and do nothing to help him. Finally, a stranger, a Samaritan, walks by and helps the man, takes him to an inn, and gives money to the innkeeper to be sure the man is well taken care of. The story of the Good Samaritan is told in response to the question, "And who is my neighbor?" Everything that follows must be seen in the context of responding to that question. This is because the story urges us to recognize that we are all to be neighbors to each other. Jesus uses a Samaritan as the central figure in this story about neighbors and love and mercy because of the deep contrast between Samaritans and Jews. Each despised the other.

The point of the story is that no one is to be excluded from the word *neighbor*.

Jesus was inviting his audience to transcend the ordinary categories of acceptable behavior. He was challenging his listeners to step into a love that was not limited by prejudice and discrimination. He was inviting them, through love, to step out of convention and into compassion.

AMAZING LOVE. As a pastor, I see many people who feel alone, isolated, defeated, useless. The truth is, everyone feels that way at times, although we don't like to admit it, except maybe to those closest to us. What we forget in those moments is that God is with us and is giving us what we need to be together and to love and to help each other. Love is truly amazing! I believe that regardless of what spiritual path you are on, when you hear this verse—"This is my commandment, love one another as I have loved you"—you can be sure that this is very good news. I have seen over and over again how this verse, when brought to awareness, can change and heal people. I think that is why, in the end, I had to write about love. *Agape* love, which starts with God, is the heart of my belief.

Rabbi Ted: Sh'ma

שְׁמַע יִשְׂרָאֵל יְהוָה אֱלֹהֵינוּ יְהוָה אֶחָד:

This is the way the *Sh'ma* looks in the Torah scroll. It is pronounced *Sh'ma Yisrael, Adonai Eloheinu, Adonai Echad,* and translated "Listen, Israel, the Eternal is our God, the Eternal is One."

THE UNEXPECTED GIFT. On a rainy December day in 1969, driving south on Highway 1 from Big Sur toward Los Angeles, I was caught in a rockslide. The mountain rose on my left, the sheer drop to the ocean was on my right, and boulders were suddenly smashing down onto my little VW Bug. In the chaos of that moment, I had my first out-of-body experience, and my life has never been the same. My previous beliefs about the nature of my being were shattered, along with the windows of my car.

Floating a considerable distance above my body, I had a unique perspective allowing the "me" in the car to avoid boulders on the highway. A silver cord reached down to the back of "my" head. Surprisingly, I felt a greater security and safety than I had ever known. I was held in a peace that I had never even imagined.

"I may be dying." The thought came with great calmness; there no longer was anything to fear. I felt totally safe.

When the car was past the rocks, I pulled off the road and suddenly snapped back into my body and into pain. I tried to shake the glass fragments from my hair, my face, and my clothes. The moment had passed, but it had rocked my belief system.

At the time, I didn't talk about my experience; it was too far outside the expected and the approved realm. I had entered a reality beyond the one I knew, and, for the first time, I knew with certainty that I was more than my physical self. I yearned to taste that freedom again—albeit, to access it less dramatically.

Did you ever notice that you only realize that you have been asleep when you awaken? It's the same with spiritual awakening. At the time of that rockslide, I thought, as a rabbi, that I already understood the word *spirituality*, but after that moment of transcendence, I realized how limited my knowledge was. Intellectually, I understood the word *spirituality* to refer to a belief in the Oneness of all Being, but it was a matter of *thought*, not of *realization*.

As I look back now, so many years later, I can appreciate how that moment fueled the expansion of my personal and professional path. My out-of-body experience during that rockslide led me to a more active focus on meditation as a gentle way to invite such moments of transcendence. At first, I learned and practiced meditative techniques from Hindu and from Zen Buddhist traditions, and then those practices actually led me to the heart of Jewish spirituality.

OLD WORDS BECOME NEW AGAIN. One of my personal prayer practices includes randomly opening a traditional *siddur*, a Jewish prayer book, to contemplate the words I find there. Not too long after my rockslide experience, I remember opening the prayer book and finding the *Sh'ma* and the *V'ahavta*, probably the most well-known parts of the Jewish worship service. At first, I was tempted to close the book and try again. After all, I had read these words thousands of times already. Instead, I tried to read them with fresh eyes.

Sh'ma Yisrael	Listen, Israel,
Adonai Eloheinu	the Eternal is our God
Adonai Echad.	the Eternal is One.
V'ahavta	And you shall love
et Adonai Elohecha	the Eternal your God
b'chol l'vavcha	with all your heart
uv'chol naf'sh'cha	with all your soul
uv'chol m'odecha.	and with all your might.
V'hayu ha-d'varim ha-eleh	And let these words
asher Anochi	which I AM
m'tzav'cha ha-yom	commanding you today
al l'vavecha.	be on your heart.

These words are central in Jewish faith. The six words of the first sentence are named after the first word, *Sh'ma,* and are referred to as the "watchword of our faith." The *Sh'ma* appears in the Book of Deuteronomy (6:4), where Moses says, "Listen, Israel, the Eternal is our God, the Eternal is One."

The text continues:

V'shinantam	And you shall repeat them
l'vanecha	to your children
v'dibarta bam	and you shall recite them
b'shiv't'cha b'vay-techa	when you sit in your house
uv'lech't'cha va-derech	and when you walk on the way
uv'shoch'b'cha	when you lie down
uv'kumecha.	and when you rise up.

I stopped there in my reading, and as I held these words in contemplation, I realized that, had I found these words in a Hindu text, I would understand them as instructions about using the verse as a mantra, a meditative focus on a word, sound, or phrase. And in that instant, with a shock of recognition, I knew that Jewish traditions of meditation existed. A path opened, and it is called the *Sh'ma*.

The *Sh'ma* is part of the traditional bedtime prayer, and the sages taught that we are to recite the *Sh'ma* at the moment of death. When asked, "But how can we know the exact moment?" they would simply repeat the instruction, as if the *Sh'ma* were to be available in consciousness always.

I began using the *Sh'ma* as the focus of my meditation, repeating the words silently and continually. I noticed how soon they appeared after I awakened in the morning and how far into sleep I could bring them at night. I carried them when I was "on my way" and when I was at home.

The *Sh'ma* serves me as foundation and as invitation, it grounds me in my tradition, and it uplifts me beyond myself. I would like to introduce you to the six words of this amazing phrase.

Sh'ma: **Listen!** It all begins with learning to listen. We are asked to be still, to release whatever current thoughts and stories, feelings and judgments, sensations and perceptions are now filling our awareness. This first word invites our silence.

There are two biblical words used to signify hearing. One of them is a verb from which the word for *ears* is derived. The other, used in this verse, has no attachment to the physical ear, so it may reflect a deeper kind of hearing.

Rabbinic commentators have noted that the Hebrew word *sh'ma* can be divided into the two-letter word *shem*, followed by the Hebrew letter *ayin*. *Shem* means "name." So one can read the word and the letter as "the name *ayin*." Since each letter of the Hebrew alphabet has a numerical equivalent, and the letter *ayin* is associated with the number seventy, this first word can be read as "the name seventy."

In the Jewish mystical tradition, there are seventy sacred names of God, so it is tempting to say that all seventy names are represented and communicated through the words of the *Sh'ma*, if one could listen well enough.

Perhaps listening itself is a spiritual path. *Sh'ma* … we are first asked to simply listen.

Yisrael: **Israel.** This Hebrew word is pronounced YISS-rah-EYL and is now known as the name of the country in the Middle East. But long before there was a country by this name, it was the name of a people, and before that, it was the name of a single person.

Jacob, the third patriarch in the Abraham, Isaac, and Jacob line, wrestled with a mysterious being before a reunion with his brother. They wrestled through the night, and even though Jacob was injured, he would not let go. His adversary said, "Let me go, for the day is breaking!" But Jacob answered, "I will not let you go, unless you bless me." Said the other, "What is your name?" He replied, "Jacob." Said he, "Your name shall no longer be Jacob, but Israel, for you have striven with beings divine and human, and have prevailed" (Genesis 32:25–28, JPS).

Drawing on an archetypal story to explain the origin of a name was common in the ancient Hebrew tradition. Here, the word *Israel* is construed to mean "one who wrestles with God." It also can mean "one who persists for God," indicating the central focus of Jewish spiritual evolution.

In the Jewish mystical tradition, the characters of the Bible are more than historical; they represent parts of us. They are metaphors and archetypes reflecting different aspects of the spiritual quest we share. In the context of the Torah, conferring the name *Israel* is a way of confirming a deeper identity on the man who began life as *Ya-akov,* or Jacob. *Ya-akov* means "the usurper," and Jacob represents the part of each of us that fears it lacks what it really needs in order to be complete.

Israel, on the other hand, represents the Greater Self manifesting itself through Jacob. This is the more inclusive identity within him, which, by its very nature, is able to "persist for God." *Israel* points to the greater, more inclusive, more connected, and more secure identity within each of us.

After the wrestling, and after the blessing, Jacob was sometimes called "Israel" and sometimes "Jacob." Like all of us, he emerged from his separate self into his greater identity, only to find himself separate once again. Just so, we open our eyes and we close our eyes; we open our *I*'s and we close our *I*'s. This is the continuing soul journey we travel. *Sh'ma Yisrael*, then, is a call to the Greater Self within each of us.

Yisrael ...

Adonai: **Eternal One.** A language develops in ways that reflect the central concern of the culture from which that language is shaped, so it is not surprising that there are a multitude of words in Hebrew for *God.* There may be, as some traditions assert, seventy different names of God, but there is one Name that is different from all the others. There is one Name of God that is never to be pronounced. This is the four-letter Name (the Hebrew letters *yod-hay-vav-hay*) called the tetragrammaton, or indicated by more traditional Jews as simply *Ha-Shem,* "The Name."

Sometime during the early days of the Second Temple, beginning in the fifth century BCE, this Name was no longer to be pronounced except once a year, and then only by the high priest. During the ritual on Yom Kippur, the Day of Atonement, the high priest alone would enter the Holy of Holies, the small chamber in the midst of the ancient Temple. With incense filling the room, he would whisper that Name only once. The community would witness this scene of great awe and mystery from the outside, but they would hear no sound.

However, since the Unspeakable Name appears so often in the Bible and in prayer texts, a tradition of substitution was developed that is still practiced today. Whenever we encounter the Unpronounceable Name, we substitute another word entirely—one word is written, but another is pronounced. When we come to this four-letter Name, we say instead the word *Adonai*, which means "Lord."

Grammatically, the four-letter Name is a form of the Hebrew verb "to be" and directs us toward the nature of all existence. This is Being unlimited by space or time; this is Being that includes all that is; this is Being that transcends all that is. *Adonai* is a spiritual path in itself, directing us toward a greater appreciation of the One in whom all else is.

Adonai ...

Eloheinu: **Our God.** The fourth word of the *Sh'ma*, pronounced *Eh-loh-HEY-nu*, literally means "our God." In biblical Hebrew, the possessive is added to the noun, so what in English would be two words appears as one. The noun itself, without the first-person plural possessive, is *Elohim* (pronounced *Eh-loh-HEEM*) and translates simply as "God."

According to the mystical commentators, *Elohim* directs us toward the One manifesting as the many. *Elohim* is identified as the *Shechinah* (pronounced *sheh-CHEE-nah*), the "indwelling Presence of God" within each of us. Our deepest identity flows from that Spark. It is the One Without Limit dwelling within us.

How can this be? How can That Which Is Without Limit dwell within each individual being? Perhaps this is the deepest Mystery of our existence. We are, in our wholeness, fully human and fully divine. Perhaps when we are most human, we are most divine, and when most divine, most fully human.

The Zohar, the thirteenth-century "bible" of the Jewish mystical tradition known as Kabbalah, teaches that *Adonai Elohim* is a complete Name: "The entire Torah in its entirety comes to teach that *Adonai Elohim* is a single Name" (vol. II, p. 161b). The Inner and the Outer, the Transcendent and the Immanent, the Universal and the Particular are One. This is the deepest truth at the heart of Jewish spiritual teaching.

From this perspective, each of us is whole, and our task is to awaken more fully to our wholeness. That awakening brings with it a clear ethic. When we are able to perceive all people as manifestations of a Single Life, we are naturally inclined to treat people with greater compassion and love. We realize that in supporting another, we are supporting ourselves; in causing pain to another, we are causing pain to ourselves. The illusion of our separateness is just that, and it is a dangerous illusion that leads us down pathways of fragmentation and alienation.

Eloheinu calls us to practice the awareness of the Universal Presence within ourselves that allows us to surrender our separate self to our Greater Identity, and urges us to live more freely and more gently on our planet.

Eloheinu …

Adonai: **Eternal One.** The Name Beyond Speech appears for a second time in this biblical verse. It looks the same, but perhaps this second appearance carries a deeper meaning.

We might imagine the progression as an evolving process. First, there is *Adonai*, the One in Whom All Else All Ways Is. Then comes the indwelling aspect of that One—the Eternal awakening within each of us as "our God"—*Eloheinu*. What might be perceived or understood or imagined as two are always One, so the progression needs to complete itself with *Adonai*. Outside and Inside are both embraced by *Adonai*. The progression allows us to understand That Which Is Never Separate from Itself. (If you're wondering why I use so many capital letters as I stretch words to contain the uncontainable, capital letters serve as reminders that these words are meant to transcend themselves.)

Adonai …

Echad: **One.** *Echad* (pronounced eh-CHAD, and it's a guttural *ch*, as in Chanukah—if you've never heard this sound, find a Jewish friend to teach it to you!) means "One." This is the basic teaching of Jewish tradition: God is One. As the awareness of this Oneness has awakened over time, many of us understand that everything that exists is a part of this One, and that nothing exists outside of this One. There is One Life, One Consciousness, One Love, One Energy that we all share. All that is, is God, but God is not limited by all that is. God is called, in the rabbinic writings of the early centuries of the Common Era, The Place (*Ha-Makom*) of the Universe. Everything is in God, and God is infinitely more than all that is.

When we approach life from this frame of reference, what has been called the golden rule, stated by various traditions either as "Do unto others as you would have them do unto you," or "Do not do to others that which is hateful to you," is not simply telling us to be nice to each other. We are to treat others as *ourselves* because we are all interconnected in the great Single Web of Being. We are to strive for that level of awareness in which Oneness is no longer a concept but a lived Reality.

Echad is the completion of the verse called the *Sh'ma. Echad* is the end and it is the beginning.

Echad ...

PUTTING IT ALL TOGETHER. Rabbi Shlomo Yitzchaki, called Rashi, the greatest of Jewish commentators, lived in eleventh-century France. He translated the *Sh'ma* this way: "Listen, Israel, *when* Adonai is our God, *then* Adonai is One." His translation acknowledges the role our own awareness plays in determining the reality of Oneness. For Rashi, the *Sh'ma* is a dynamically evolving teaching.

The *Sh'ma* is an invitation to the Greater Territory of our own awareness. The *Sh'ma* is more than a statement of Reality, it is a gateway to that Reality. The *Sh'ma* is itself a Way.

Sh'ma ...

Sheikh Jamal: Basmala

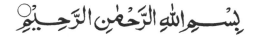

Bismillah ir Rahman ir Rahim

The heart of the Qur'an is said to be encoded in the formula called *Basmala*. The words of the *Basmala* are *Bismillah ir Rahman ir Rahim*, meaning "In the name of God, boundlessly Compassionate and Merciful." The *Basmala* opens all but one of the 114 chapters of the Qur'an. In a famous *Hadith*, the collected sayings of the Prophet Muhammad, the Prophet said that all that is in the revealed books is contained in the Qur'an, all that is in the Qur'an is contained in the opening chapter called *Fatiha*, and all that is in the *Fatiha* is contained in the *Basmala*.

ORIGIN AND MEANING OF **BASMALA**. The first word of the *Basmala*—*Bismillah*—means "In the name of Allah." *Allah*, the Arabic word for God, is derived from the Canaanite *Allat* or *Elat*, the Hebrew *Elohim*, and the Aramaic *Alaha*. There are two root words involved: *Al* or *El*, meaning "Sacred Everything," and *La*, meaning "Sacred Nothing." This fusion of everything and nothing is Allah, God, the ultimate mystery.

The Qur'an says that we cannot understand the essence of God with our human faculties. Better, says the Holy Book, to contemplate the divine qualities: "To God belong the most beautiful names" (59:24). Of the ninety-nine divine names mentioned in the Qur'an, most frequently cited are *Rahman* (Compassion) and *Rahim* (Mercy), the other core words of the *Basmala*. Occurring more than two hundred times in the Holy Book, these two names convey the unmistakable message that compassion is not only a primary quality of God, it is God's very essence.

Both *rahman* and *rahim* are derived from an old Middle Eastern Semitic root, *rhm*, which refers to an emanation from a deep interior. In Hebrew the word *rechem* means "womb," and both *rahman* and *rahim* suggest the function of a womb. As applied to God, *rahman*, with an active *-an* ending, is the creative aspect of this womblike compassion, while *rahim*, with its passive *-im* ending, is the receptive aspect. In spiritual language, *Rahman* is the Sun of Compassion and *Rahim* the Moon of Compassion.

If the core of Divinity is Compassion and God is all-powerful, does that mean that compassion is ultimate strength? Does it mean that the most empowered person is the one who is the most compassionate? Yes! In the Qur'an, the metaphor for compassion in nature is water. Water is soft, gentle, and yielding. But, unleashed in torrents, it has the power to wash away continents. Compassion is authentic strength. Even more amazing, the Qur'an points out, is that "We made from water every living thing" (21:30). Wherever water falls, life flourishes. When the earth is parched, says the Qur'an, and God sends down the waters of Mercy, "forthwith the earth is clothed in green" (22:63). Thus, not only is the attribute of compassion filled with power, it is also life-affirming and life-bestowing.

COMPASSION FOR SELF. A beautiful secret of the *Basmala* is that on our journey to know God, we are seeking to know our own innermost self, a divine self that reveals itself only in the womb of compassion. In the imagery of the Qur'an, our "water and clay" forms are infused with the breath of God. Sufi teachers point out that in our quest to arrive at our "real name," we often encounter bewildering contradictions and mysteries. By exercising compassion for our complexities, we create an inner spaciousness that allows the bewildering paradoxes to play themselves out and reveal their place in God's plan for us. By practicing compassion for self, we begin to connect with our divine essence. In other words, compassion for self is the key to discovering God's name inside us.

In a *Hadith*, God says: "Between you and Me, there are seventy thousand veils; but between Me and you, there are no veils." Our work is to remove the veils. "Marry your soul," says Rumi, "that wedding is the Way." This is the work of aligning our personality to our higher self. When we accept our longings and bewilderment with compassion, deeper truths emerge organically and our divine identity asserts itself.

Once the work of transforming the little self is under way, a cry from within bubbles up to the surface of our consciousness: "O my Sustainer! Open up my heart to Thy Light!" (20:25, trans. Asad). We become aware at an experiential level that Divine Heart is in human heart. In a *Hadith Qudsi,* a sacred saying of the Prophet based on an insight directly revealed by God to him, usually through a dream, Allah says, "I cannot be contained in the space of the earth; I cannot be contained in the space of the heavens; but I can be contained in the space of the pure loving heart of my servant." Between human heart and Divine Heart lie many levels of consciousness and realization. Rumi asks us to spare no effort in opening a window from heart to Heart because "the Moon will kiss you only through the window."

And how do we open the window of our heart? There is the invaluable work of purifying our being and also the discipline of meditation and silence. These two practices bring us closer to the Divine Heart. But the essential work is to embrace not only the ten thousand joys of life but also its ten thousand sorrows, always invoking the *Basmala*.

Unpleasant feelings, such as sadness or anger, are just energies that are begging to be acknowledged and integrated. The Qur'an states that it is God who has created feelings and caused our laughter and tears (23:78 and 53:36). In other words, they are all sacred and by acknowledging our feelings—our laughter and our tears—we are honoring the All-Merciful. When we avoid or deny them, we are creating stone walls around our hearts and closing ourselves off from Divine Heart. But when we embrace them gently, with compassion for ourselves and, little by little, through a practice my grandfather called "sacred holding" (which I describe further in chapter 6), we allow them to be integrated and healed. When with courage and compassion we kiss our dragons, they turn into princes and princesses. Our hearts expand, the windows open, and we take a giant step toward union with the Beloved.

COMPASSION FOR OTHERS. Once we cultivate compassion for self and come closer to our essential self, we become aware that we need to invoke the *Basmala* in our relationship with others. Every person is precious to God. The Qur'an says, "Everywhere you turn is the Face of Allah" (2:115).

Our true names are not just our personalities, formed by our conditioned reactions to life circumstances, but also the gift of the Divine Breath bestowed on each of us. We need to make a distinction between behavior and being, between form and essence. Our behaviors might sometimes be evil, but our being, or essence, is never evil. Regardless of our offenses, inside each one of us resides a divine nature—call it Divine Breath, Christ Nature, *Elohim* Essence, or any other sacred name that speaks to you.

The art of invoking the *Basmala* in relating to others is, for me, epitomized in the sage advice offered by the fifteenth-century mystic Kabir that we should do what is right but never leave the person's being out of our heart. When we encounter someone who is harmful or offensive, of course we need to do "what is right" to protect ourselves and prevent the abuse. But at the same time, we must make every effort to keep that person's essence in our heart. This may be hard to do, but we must remind ourselves again and again that we are fighting the antagonism, not the antagonist. Just the sheer energy of this awareness and discernment, as it informs our actions, has the power to shift heaven and earth.

To illustrate this critical point, my Sufi teachers gave the example of two judges meting out a life sentence to a violent offender. One judge, operating on the level of his own ego, is eager to banish that "scum of the earth" to oblivion and issues the sentence with disdain and contempt. This judge makes no distinction between behavior and being. The other judge, speaking from a more compassionate and prayerful heart, reads the life sentence with solemnity but not disdain, and attempts to ensure that the offender is not maltreated in prison. Such a judge distinguishes between behavior and being, recognizing the true, sacred name of the offender. Though the life sentence is the same in both cases, it is delivered with two different energies: one from the ego, the other from the soul. Just this distinction can have a surprisingly profound impact on the world.

Remembering that God's essence is compassion and mercy, when we speak and act in justice we are expressing our consciousness of the highest form of compassion and mercy. In the name of God, in the spirit of *Basmala*, we must be compassionate to those in need, feeding the hungry and assuaging the pain of the afflicted.

On a deeper level, we most truly honor the Divine Breath in us and cherish the Divine Heart in our human hearts when we liberate the poor, the hungry, and the afflicted from the bondage of our own prejudices, exploitation, greed, and indifference. This is the truly steep path of virtue mentioned in the Qur'an. It requires us to gather our courage, increase our awareness, and expand our compassion so that we can work in God's name to make systemic changes in our society and create shifts within ourselves to "free a bondsman" and create justice for the disenfranchised (90:11).

A SECRET TREASURE. In a beautiful revelation to the Prophet, God said, "I was a secret Treasure and I longed to be known, and so I created the worlds, visible and invisible." I believe that God's longing to be known is cosmically embedded in every human heart, and sooner or later we shall feel and act on this deep inner ache. We are not always aware of this longing, spiritual teachers tell us, because it is obscured by the veils of health and wealth. When our health is sound and our emotional and financial situations are secure, all this talk about God and spirituality might feel irrelevant and inconvenient. But should one of those veils be torn away, we suddenly awaken and begin to ask deeper questions. We seek divine help, and our lives become, in one form or another, a journey to God. Along the way we discover a God of infinite compassion and mercy.

At first blush, this seems untrue. How could a compassionate God allow the Holocaust to happen, brutal wars to continue, natural disasters to occur, tyrants to retain power, and bad things to happen to good people? To these questions, there is no satisfactory answer. I take refuge in the Qur'an's statement that we are given but a little knowledge (17:85) and in Rumi's insight, "Sell your cleverness and buy bewilderment."

But the greater mystery to me is this: Some of the people I find the most joyous and spiritual are those who have gone through the most difficult tragedies in their lives. In the journey of transforming their curses into blessings, they have developed faith in a God filled with infinite goodness and mercy. In the process, their beings have become graced by joy and hope.

I believe that a true understanding of the *Basmala* can only come from personal experience. It cannot be embraced by words or explained by logic. In my own life, paradoxically, I experienced divine compassion most exquisitely in my time of greatest sorrow.

One March evening in 1991, in a state of anguish, I meditated and prayed fervently for God to save my mother's life. Only five days earlier my mother had arrived in Seattle from Bangladesh on a hastily arranged trip that she insisted upon. Early the first morning after she arrived she began to vomit blood and was rushed to a local hospital. From there a helicopter flew her to Harborview, a trauma hospital, where she lay critically ill. Our family—my father and younger sister in Bangladesh, my brother who accompanied my mother to Seattle, and I—were in a state of shock. It was inconceivable that our mother's life was ebbing away. She was only sixty years old and had so many plans and hopes. Our hearts thrashed and quivered like fish out of water.

After four agonizing days and nights, it was clear that the situation was desperate. We needed help. Not any ordinary help—we needed help from a Higher Source.

The Qur'an says that God, the Lord of Grace unbounded, answers the prayers of the supplicant. Many of my parents' teachings flooded into my mind. When there is an "increased necessity," they used to say, God provides. When a child is born, the mother's breasts are magically filled with milk.

My motivation was of cosmic proportions. In my prayers and meditation that evening I was going to plumb the depths of my soul, and from there cry out to God to save my mother's life. In the words of Rumi, "I shall cry to Thee and cry to Thee until the milk of Thy loving-kindness boils over."

In the early hours of the morning, I found myself coming out through portal after portal of consciousness from a depth of Mystery that amazed me. As I was coming into consciousness, I heard myself shouting at the top of my voice with a decibel of loudness that could be heard for miles. Quickly I realized that this super-screaming must be an internal voice, for everyone in the house was still fast asleep. Even more surprising than the shouting were the words I was using: a volley of four-letter words that are not in my normal vocabulary. And then I was shocked to realize that I was hurling these shameful epithets at some aspect of Divinity! But the shocker of shockers was that I did not feel one iota of guilt or remorse for my sacrilegious behavior—on the contrary, I experienced an unspeakable sense of intimacy, of closeness and bonding with Mystery.

It was a marvelous phenomenon to experience such an indescribable closeness in the very midst of my profanity. In a state of wonder, I distinctly heard the rustling of wings and felt a wave of compassion and peace descending on me. At that moment every cell of my being dissolved into a sweetness that mystics have described as existing "before honey or bee."

But the story doesn't end there. Within a few days, my mother passed away. Because in Muslim tradition, burial needs to occur within twenty-four hours, there was no way for my father to arrive in time. Instead, he remained in Bangladesh, where, in his grief, he plunged himself into a dizzying burst of activities, hurriedly trying to complete projects he had begun in the villages of northern Bengal. As a retired ambassador he had connections and clout, and he used them vigorously to pursue what the Qur'an calls "righteous deeds." Then he traveled to his ancestral village and astonished the villagers by supervising the digging of his own grave next to that of his parents in the ancestral graveyard. After completing a round of farewells to the living and visiting the graves of departed loved ones, he simply willed himself to die. My parents had been married for forty-two years and were remarkably bonded as a couple. His death certificate cites a massive heart attack as the cause of death, but really, my father died of a broken heart.

We three children were stunned by the sudden turn of events. The enormity of our loss was difficult to fathom. How could it be that suddenly both Mother and Father were gone forever from this existence? We had been a very close-knit family, and now we were being ripped asunder!

Surprisingly, my intense grief meshed with a strange celebration. In the depths of my being I knew the truth of Allah's blessing in the Qur'an: "O soul, in complete rest and satisfaction! Return to your Sustainer well-pleased and well-pleasing! Enter then among my devoted ones! Yes, enter my Garden!" (89:27–30, trans. Helminski). Strengthened and supported by that mystical experience of the *Basmala*, I knew that my beloved mother and father were soaring in divine meadows. The exquisite insight of Rumi about death danced in my heart: a lovesick nightingale caught the fragrance of roses and, breaking free of its cage, flew away to the rose garden.

Out of this profound experience, my understanding of the *Basmala* has been expansive and heartfelt. From the depth of my being I now know that God is boundlessly compassionate and intimately close to each one of us. No matter how far I stray or transgress, my compassionate Sustainer takes care of me, just as the ocean takes care of every wave. No matter what event befalls me, it is part of a divine plan that may be a mystery to me but exists in the compassionate mind of the Creator.

For me, the key to fulfillment is living the *Basmala*. A Bedouin once entreated the Prophet to tell him how he could invite God's boundless compassion to be bestowed on him. The Prophet replied, "Have compassion on yourself and on others, and Infinite compassion will be given to you."

Finding Common Ground

As the three of us listened to each other describe a central text that informs our faith and our life, it became clear that there were both similarities and differences among our traditions. As we focused, we were better able to identify the uniqueness of our own traditions. But we were also better able to see how much we had in common.

We were struck by the fact that each tradition speaks words of healing and wholeness: *oneness, love,* and *compassion.* The basic teaching of Judaism focuses on One God. Christianity brought a central focus on love to a larger world. And Islam, in its emphasis on compassion, incorporated much of the richness of Jewish and Christian teachings and brought them to a population that had largely been untouched by them. Oneness is the ground on which love awakens, and from this ground compassion is born. Each teaching is crucial, and each is intertwined with the others.

We had thought that each of our faiths had a core teaching meant for the world, and surely we confirmed this. But we also learned that our core teachings are meant for us. We Jews need to learn more profoundly the lessons of oneness to counter feelings of alienation and separateness. We Christians are in need of our own teachings of love to counteract a history of exclusion and violence. And we Muslims are in need of the very deep teachings of compassion that our tradition teaches.

In seeking a central teaching, we not only provided enrichment for each other, but confirmed for ourselves what we are striving to learn. As we inquired more deeply into our traditions, our dialogue expanded, and we were far better able to appreciate the wisdom each of us expressed. How different our world would look if we could all embrace these ideals in our daily lives!

It may well be that each of us can find a central principle that we consider most important in our lives. You might find that there is a particular value that you consider reflects the nature of the current spiritual path you are traveling. Sometimes seeking and sharing such a core value can not only help you understand yourself more fully, but also appreciate another's values. If you are ready to embark on the work of stage 3 and want to inquire more deeply into your own faith, if you want to share your beliefs with someone from another faith tradition, remember that you need to establish an environment of mutual respect. The goal is a deeper understanding and appreciation, not determining who is "right." You are each entrusting the other with your deeply held beliefs, and it is a time for listening, not questioning; for honoring, not challenging. You might find it very interesting to see how each of your core values speak to one another!

4

THE PROMISES AND PROBLEMS OF OUR TRADITIONS

Sharing Both the Easy and the Difficult Parts

Honest Dialogue

We have looked at the stories we have shared to move beyond the energies of suspicion and separation. We have engaged in a deeper inquiry, hoping to provide you with a more appreciative understanding of our three faith traditions. But, as always, there is more to the story. There are things that we might rather *not* share with one another, either because we are uncomfortable with them ourselves or because we imagine that others will be uncomfortable with them. Yet, if we are to encourage deeper and more honest dialogue, these are exactly the things we need to share with each other.

Once the three of us began working together, it became clear that a deeper personal relationship was developing. As happens in all relationships, we began to notice not only our similarities but also our differences. We saw Pastor Don as a master of current culture, able to connect appropriate lines from authors and films to the substance of his theological teaching. Sheikh Jamal seemed to be a modern incarnation of Rumi, able to bring forth lines of poetry from that master, along with precise quotes from the Qur'an and other teachings of Islam. And we had come to expect that Rabbi Ted was likely to express his teachings of Torah and Jewish tradition through metaphors of psychology and spirituality.

Differences in personality and personal style sometimes help and sometimes challenge any meaningful relationship. Pastor Don is more thoughtful, organized, and meticulous than his fellow amigos. Rabbi Ted tends to get upset more quickly, yet is then often able to utilize those upsets in the service of greater learning and fuller teaching. Sheikh Jamal is the calmest of us, able to move beyond surface distractions and maintain an open heart.

As we continued to share both professionally and personally, through many hours of spiritual direction, it became clear to us that there were incredibly beautiful teachings springing from each of our traditions. But there were also problem texts that caused confusion and difficulty for us—and for many who tried to understand our faiths. We knew that our religious traditions contained both light and shadow, just as each of us contain both as human beings. There were many moments when we encountered texts and beliefs that were uncomfortable to discuss. We are, for example, representatives of the three Abrahamic faiths, but we understand Abraham in very different ways. For Rabbi Ted, Abraham was the first of the three patriarchs of Jewish tradition; for Sheikh Jamal, Abraham was the first Muslim. Both Judaism and Islam have a familial connection to Abraham through his sons, Isaac and Ishmael. For Pastor Don, Abraham is the first person of faith, but any familial connection is complicated by the legacy of Christian anti-Judaism.

At the beginning, Ted was uncomfortable with the exact wording from the Qur'an that states, "Abraham was not a Jew, nor a Christian, but he was true in faith and bowed his will to Allah's [which is Islam], and he joined not gods with Allah [he was not a polytheist]" (3:67). While Jamal was quick to explain that *Muslim* simply means "one who submits to God," it did not sit well with Ted to find Abraham declared a Muslim and not a Jew. Pastor Don, appreciating Rabbi Ted's dilemma, said, "You've already been told by Christians that your faith is incomplete, and now you are being told by Muslims the same thing."

These are realities that, like them or not, are part of our interfaith life together. The entire interfaith journey involves appreciating the impact of such verses on others and moving toward a greater appreciation of their historical context. As our relationship deepened, it became easier to confront together the difficulties we experienced with some aspects of our own faith traditions, and to discuss issues we had with each other's texts.

To be able to share freely, to be heard, and to be open to greater understanding with the "difficult stuff" requires a relationship of trust. It takes honesty, humility, and a willingness to be vulnerable with another person to get to this level of relationship. There is no more room—or need—for pretense. This is the stage where we can each hear what the other has to say with an open heart. This is stage 3 in the process of getting to the heart of interfaith: sharing both the easy and the difficult parts of our faiths.

It is a stage of willingness to share the dilemmas that our traditions pose for us, and for others. It is a stage of freely admitting that no spiritual path is without its exclusionist claims. It is a stage of openness to speak about misunderstandings and misinterpretations. It can also be a stage of tremendous growth: bringing these matters candidly to each other allows communication to deepen and permits our understanding to expand.

As you read our disclosures about the promises and problems we each find in our traditions, our hope is that you will be encouraged to bring to light aspects of your own tradition with which you have difficulty.

Pastor Don: What I Am Uncomfortable with in the Christian Tradition

The belief that Christianity is the only way. "I am the way, the truth, and the life. No one comes to the Father except through me"

(John 14:6). There it is. There are several ways to interpret these words, but the verses have contributed strongly to the exclusive stance of Christians. Other verses also suggest exclusivity, such as Matthew 28:19: "Go therefore and make disciples of all nations, baptizing them in the name of the Father and of the Son and of the Holy Spirit, and teaching them to obey everything that I have commanded you." Some verses are more vulnerable to the perception of exclusivity than others. In actuality, the more exclusive a verse *seems* to be, the more dependent it is on being defined by someone's need to fulfill and protect the self.

I have my own interpretations of these verses, but many people have used them to justify not just exclusivity, but violence and hatred—things wholly inconsistent with the Gospel message of Jesus. So I don't like that these verses exist in a way that leaves them open to such narrow interpretation. But part of being a person of faith is to carry the challenge of verses like these. I'm reminded of Gandhi's statement that every religion contains truth and untruth. I believe that we each have to face the "untruths" of our tradition. And, for me, this idea that Christianity is the only authentic spiritual path is an untruth.

The teachings of some about the inequality of women. "Wives be subject to your husbands" (Ephesians 5:22). It is impossible today to know exactly what it felt like to be a woman in the early days of the church. But we have evidence that women were treated with far more honor and respect in those early days of the church than this verse from Paul's letter to the church at Ephesus would suggest. The Book of Acts, for example, uses phrases such as "both men and women" that seem to be self-consciously pointing toward equality (Acts 5:14 and Acts 8:12). Nonetheless, this one verse from Ephesians has been used to force women into a role subservient to men and has been the cause of unhappiness and lost opportunities for fulfillment. It has also been a root of domestic violence. For me, the idea that women should be second-class citizens is an untruth.

The prohibitions against homosexuality. "For this reason God gave them up to degrading passions. Their women exchanged natural intercourse for unnatural, and in the same way also the men, giving up natural intercourse with women, were consumed with passion for one another" (Romans 1:26–27a). Although homosexuality is never mentioned by that name in the Bible, and although Jesus never talks about it, people have often used verses like these to brand homosexuality as a sin. But almost all the biblical references condemning homosexual behavior point toward activities that interrupt or damage existing relationships between men and women. Seen in the context of love, homosexuality sustained by a loving relationship is not a threat to society and fulfills a particular sexual orientation. I believe the idea that homosexuality is a sin is an untruth.

The prohibitions against divorce. "But I say to you, anyone who divorces his wife, except on grounds of unchastity, causes her to commit adultery; and whoever marries a divorced woman commits adultery" (Matthew 5:32). The critical issue concerning divorce is the same as the issue involving homosexuality: It needs to be understood in the context of love. The preciousness of a relationship is sustainable only with a focus on the concerns of the other and requires a spirituality capable of rising above the ordinary needs of the self. But who can do this all the time? And yet, the narrower interpretation of this verse has been to suggest that divorce is not only a sin, it is shameful. While divorce is tragic and sad, it is also a reality of being human and can be accepted with love and dignity and compassion. I believe the idea that divorce is a sin is an untruth.

The attitudes toward Jews. "For this reason, the Jews were seeking all the more to kill him" (John 5:18a). Frequent New Testament references to "the Jews," especially in the Gospel of John, convey an attempt to demonize Jews. By the time the Gospel of John was written, Christianity was trying to define itself in juxtaposition to its perceived enemies: Gnostics, Pagans, and Jews. These references to "the Jews" seem to deny the reality that Jesus was a Jew, a teacher, and probably a rabbi, and that the disciples of Jesus were also Jews. The way the phrase *the Jews* is used furthers a "we-they" relationship between Christians and Jews and has been used to justify the persecution of Jews by Christians over the centuries. That behavior is completely inconsistent with "Love one another as I have loved you." The sense that Jews were responsible for the death of Jesus, or that they are any more "evil" than anyone else, is an untruth.

Each of these verses that I don't like points to an exclusivism, a "we-they" sensibility, and a focus that is not consistent with the commandment to "Love one another as I have loved you." These difficult verses challenge me to think critically about them, to listen carefully to those who understand them differently, and to work always toward the loving community that I believe I am called to with all people. Sometimes, these verses even call me to be tolerant of intolerance.

Pastor Don: What I Am Grateful for in the Christian Tradition

The emphasis on love. Love is the essence of oneness, and that is Jesus's recurring theme. The high value placed on love, and the ways in which love can make real the oneness that Jesus preached from his tradition of Judaism, give life and hope to all that Jesus taught and did. The emphasis on love has a solid connection to Judaism and leads to compassion, which is so important to Islam. Jesus taught that when we act out of love, we live out a level of spiritual awareness that lifts us to a place where we can see and feel how love can reshape us into people capable of establishing and maintaining loving community. This is a truth of Christianity.

The emphasis on healing. There are many stories about Jesus's healing miracles in the Gospels. What is important about those stories is not so much the details of individual lives being healed, but the broad interest Jesus has in making use of the power of his spirit for the healing of community. Personal healing without any thought of the larger community almost always runs the risk of moving to the excesses of individualism. Healing is about being made to feel whole, and that's where the word *salvation* comes from. *Salving* means to "make whole."

But the healing Jesus uses for those individuals points to something much broader and more hopeful. Jesus's healing ministry encourages us to *wake up,* to come to a place where our self-understanding has a profoundly positive effect on how we feel, how we act, and how we think. Self-understanding can deepen our awareness of how we are connected to God and to each other. It can also help us realize that we have more control over that bigger picture than we might have thought: we can play a responsible role in our healing as spiritual people.

God's intention for healing for all of creation made known in Jesus is a truth of Christianity.

The challenge to the status quo. *Challenge* is far too mild a word to describe Jesus's message. It was both offensive and scandalous to those who wished to preserve the status quo. When he overturned the tables of the moneychangers who were exchanging Roman coins and other foreign currency for the Temple shekels, he was justifiably angry. He saw how the management of the Temple had drifted from drawing people closer to God into preserving the status quo for the wealthy. His actions spoke volumes about the depth of his convictions about love and justice. He was truly a prophet who, acting out of love, saw something wrong and expressed his anguish and grief to help shape awareness and encourage response.

Jesus consistently emphasized the value of loving community. In his teachings called the Sermon on the Mount, Jesus challenged conventions that persistently supported the needs of the self and not the greater good and portrayed a new vision of how life could be different. The golden rule, to "do to others as you would have them do to you" (Matthew 7:12), and the commandment to "love your enemies and pray for those who persecute you" (Matthew 7: 43, 44) call for a much higher level of spiritual awareness and a commitment to the kind of community that level of awareness can generate. Jesus's challenge to the status quo is a truth of Christianity.

The power of the resurrection of Jesus. Every Sunday, Christian worship is a celebration of the resurrection of Jesus. While that gives shape and substance to our worship, far too much time and energy have been spent on whether or not the resurrection really happened. For me, through eyes of love and faith, it did. But far more important than that is what the story of the resurrection points to. It shows us a picture of life where redemption, forgiveness, and reconciliation shape a world of love and not fear. As St. Francis said of his ministry, "We have come to heal wounds, to bind up the brokenhearted, and to bring home those who have lost their way." For Christians, the resurrection, a making real of the power of God in Jesus, points to a world where healing has been accomplished and where we have, today, exactly what we need to experience that. The resurrection expresses this vital truth of Christianity, that God can make all things new.

Pastor Don: What I Want Others to Know about Christianity

Christianity is rooted in Judaism. Christianity does not take the place of Judaism. Jesus was Jewish and a rabbi, a teacher. His work was another attempt to bring to fruition the message and promise of oneness first made known during the Exodus from Egypt. His message makes no sense without Judaism.

Christians believe that Jesus was anointed (hence the word *Christ* from the Greek *Christos*, which means "anointed one," "messiah"): "God anointed Jesus of Nazareth with the Holy Spirit and with power ... for God was with him" (Acts 10:38). In other words, we believe that Jesus was imbued with energy and resources by God for a specific purpose. But for what purpose? I think Jesus was imbued with power to make real the substance of Judaism: oneness. Jesus was designated to become a prophet in the great Jewish tradition of prophecy to challenge the status quo. Jesus was called to help with healing—the healing of persons, the healing of community, the healing of all of creation. God was *in* Jesus to do all these things.

Early Christianity was truer to Jesus's teachings. A close reading of the Book of Acts reveals that the people who were among the first followers of Jesus tried very hard to live their lives according to the teachings in the Gospels. Three items stand out. First, there was a genuine attempt to understand and practice equality between men and women: Acts 2:17 refers to both "your sons and your daughters." Second, there was an attempt to hold material goods in common, a sharing of material wealth: "All who believed were together and had all things in common; they would sell their possessions and distribute the proceeds to all, as any had need" (Acts 2:44, 45). And, third, there was an adherence to nonviolent resistance, as evidenced in the story of the stoning of Stephen, who cried out, "Lord, do not hold this sin against them" when he died (Acts 7:59, 60).

Much of this finally came to an end at the Council of Nicea in 325 CE, when Christianity was given legal status in the Roman Empire. The fact that life today in Christian communities does not fully reflect Jesus's teachings is partly a matter of the fusion of Christianity and the Roman Empire nearly two millennia ago. While the substance of Christianity would not support empire, the practice of Christianity became domesticated enough to embrace the status quo and, therefore, became useful to the empire. Christian people have yet to recover from that, yet I hold these early church practices as evidence of the core of what Jesus taught.

Rabbi Ted: What Troubles Me in the Jewish Tradition

The belief that we are God's only chosen people. "How odd of God to choose the Jews." I don't know where that line came from, but I often think of it when confronting the issue of chosenness. From one point of view, that choice seems to have led to a great deal of hardship; the history of the Jews is replete with suffering. From another point of view, this is the essential claim of exclusivity within Jewish tradition: God chose us and not you; we are the special people.

> For you are a people consecrated to the Eternal your God.
> Of all the peoples on earth the Eternal your God chose you
> to be His treasured people.
>
> *Deuteronomy 7:6*

Because being a Jew is essentially a tribal affiliation, this special characteristic of the Jewish community might seem to be reflected in Jewish culture. I certainly grew up being taught that there was something special about being a Jew, that we had some kind of special relationship with the Divine. But this specialness has too often promoted an exclusivism that, I believe, is hurtful both to Jews and to others.

Once, just before officiating at the wedding of friends I met in graduate school, I discovered that a cousin of the bride was a very traditional rabbi. I approached him and invited him to share in the ceremony. Although he was ultra-Orthodox, we shared the same marriage blessings. His response was immediate and negative: he would not participate with me, because I did not observe Judaism as he did. I told him that it was sad that a tradition meant to unite us wound up creating such separations, and his response was again sharp and quick.

"Tradition is not meant to unite us," he said, "it's meant to differentiate between those who are doing it right and those who are not."

This judgmental quality is difficult for those of us celebrating a more universal message within Jewish tradition. And as far as being the Chosen People is concerned, I believe that we are *a* chosen people, but not *the* chosen people. I believe that each people is chosen for their own way. The Jewish Way is called Torah; Jews are chosen for the Way called Torah. Christians, Muslims, and all other authentic spiritual communities are equally chosen for the integrity of their Way. Too often we imagine that there is just one Way, and that always leads to difficulties.

The violence. I grew up hearing that the God of the Old Testament (what we call either the Hebrew Bible, the Hebrew Scriptures, or the Tanach) is a violent God, and the God of the New Testament is a loving God. And while there are many examples of the love and compassion of God in Hebrew Scriptures, the violent side of God is clearly expressed. Sometimes, in fact, God sounds pretty darn angry.

> Thus said the Eternal One of Hosts: "I am exacting the penalty for what Amalek did to Israel, for the assault he made upon them on the road, on their way up from Egypt. Now go, attack Amalek, and destroy all that belongs to him. Spare no one, but kill alike men and women, infants and sucklings, oxen and sheep, camels and asses!"
>
> *1 Samuel 15:2–3, JPS*

There are so many stories of violence in the Bible, it is almost impossible to pick out only a few to illustrate this aspect of an ancient tradition. Sometimes I am not surprised by the violence and the cruelty, but by the astonishing spiritual clarity of other passages. There is no way to avoid the serious violence called for, as well as accomplished by, the God of the Hebrew Scriptures. I can remind myself of the differences in culture between our time and theirs, but then I see the extent of violence in our world and realize that we are not so different from our ancestors after all. Revenge, hatred, and violence are simply a part of life, a part of our development as human beings. We had as much trouble with those in the past as we do now.

I do not enjoy being reminded of this part of myself. I do not enjoy projecting this violence onto the Divine. But I understand it, and I understand how it has impacted our people and our world. The violent anger that is attributed to God is also part of the issue of a God who rewards and punishes us for our behavior.

The view of God as the Rewarder and Punisher. It is our basic nature to know the world through comparison. We know hard in contrast to soft, warm in contrast to cold, love in contrast to hate, happiness in contrast to sadness. We also know reward in contrast to punishment. It is this paradigm that I find so difficult in my tradition: the idea that God loves us when we are good and does not love us when we are bad; that God rewards us when we are good and punishes us when we are bad.

Some of the verses in Deuteronomy, for example, are very difficult for me:

> Now, if you obey the Eternal your God, to carefully keep all His commandments which I enjoin upon you this day, the Eternal your God will set you high above all the nations of the earth.... But if you do not obey the Eternal your God ... all these curses shall come upon you.... The Eternal will let loose against you calamity, panic, and frustration in all the enterprises you undertake, so that you shall soon be utterly wiped out because of your evildoing in forsaking Me.... If you fail to observe faithfully all the terms of this Teaching that are written in this book ... the Eternal will inflict extraordinary plagues upon you and your offspring, strange and lasting plagues, malignant and chronic diseases.
>
> *28:1, 15, 20, 58, 59, JPS*

This is not the loving God who appears elsewhere in scripture, but the reflection of a part of ourselves that operates through punishing or rewarding. These verses maintain that the reason for honoring the commandments is to obtain blessing and avoid destruction, rather than observing principles of living that increase our joy and fulfillment. These verses of reward and punishment support those who perceive the God of the Hebrew Scriptures as an angry and punishing deity.

Even though I understand these verses to be reflections of less spiritual parts of ourselves, the verses are still difficult to deal with. I do not believe in this kind of god. I do not believe that God's love for us is dependent on our performance. Indeed, the difference between God's love and most human love is that God's love is unconditional. God loves us always. It is we who are either open or closed to that Love in any given moment.

Rabbi Ted: What I Am Grateful for in the Jewish Tradition

The belief that every being is an expression of One.

It has been clearly shown to you that the Eternal One alone is God; there is nothing else.

Deuteronomy 4:35

At its heart, Judaism reflects an ongoing, evolving quest to understand and to celebrate the Oneness of God. Through the ages, our understanding of this One has changed. At first, that One was imagined to be "out there" somewhere. Divine beings, in early biblical days, were associated with high places—each mountain might have its own deity.

As Judaism developed, a theology called monolatrism—in which many deities existed, but only One was powerful and worthy of praise—took root in the early patriarchal period. This was a stage toward the development of true monotheism, in which no other gods are acknowledged: there is only One, and that One is God of all peoples.

The exclusivity of Israel's relationship with God gave way to a more universal awareness. The same God who freed the children of Israel from Egypt freed others from their times of enslavement. This was a major moment in the unfolding quest for Oneness. Through the ages, Jewish scholars have probed the nature of this One as the distance between God and person began to decrease. In the flowering of eighteenth-century Hasidism, that distance is bridged, and the ancient words of Torah announcing "there is nothing else" are taken literally. It's not just that there is no other God; it's that there is nothing but God. Everything that exists is God, yet God is infinitely more than everything. This evolution of Oneness unveils greater levels of inclusivity. All of life is sacred because everything is infused with One Life. We are led to seek paths of compassion and peace because we recognize that Life in every person we meet.

Sometimes, when speaking or leading a workshop and talking about this reality of One, I ask people to count off. You know, where someone begins with "One," the next says, "Two," and so on. But before the second person can go to "Two," I tell them that they are also to count themselves as "One." Everyone is "One." After the counting is done, I encourage folks to remember, whenever they see another person, "There goes another *one!*" People usually get a chuckle out of this, but I am hopeful that they also see the point and perhaps remember that we are all truly One.

The teaching that every person is holy.

> The Eternal One spoke to Moses, saying, "Speak to the whole Israelite community and say to them: You shall be holy, for I, the Eternal your God, am holy."
>
> *Leviticus 19:1–2*

I value the Jewish teaching that human beings carry holiness within them, that we are the messengers of the Divine on earth, the hands of God, able to support and to soothe and to heal. Each human being has a God-given dignity that needs to be discovered, honored, and expressed.

We are also beings with free choice, without which our compassionate actions would have no meaning. We are free to realize our true identity as a unique expression of the Divine or to ignore it. We are free to heal or to hurt. We have the dignity as well as the responsibility of choice.

And because human beings reflect that holiness as part of the One Life, the One Being, the One Reality, we are called on to care for ourselves and each other in compassionate and loving ways. The poor and the stranger are to be comforted and supported. The closest word the Hebrew language has to the English word *charity* is *tzedakah*, which actually means "righteousness." Giving to those in need is not understood simply as a charitable act; it is an essential act of righteousness.

The prophet Micah encapsulated in these words what is asked of each of us:

> It has been told you, humankind, what is good, and what the Eternal One asks of you: Only to do justly, and love with loving-kindness, and to walk in integrity with your God.
>
> *Micah 6:8*

This is part of what I am so very grateful for in my Jewish tradition. We are evolving to transcend ourselves. Everything flows from the recognition and the realization of Oneness. If there is a single gift that the Jews have given to the world, it is this: that there is One God, One Life, One Being. We are contained in that Life and we are expressions of that Life. And we are striving to live that Oneness into our world, to exemplify that sense of divine Oneness in our lives.

Rabbi Ted: What I Want Others to
Know about Judaism

Jewish tradition keeps evolving. There seems to be a common misconception that Judaism somehow stopped with the "Old Testament." But, in truth, Judaism has always evolved with a rhythm between written Torah and oral Torah. Once a text is written down, it becomes the basis for the discussions, stories, and principles that spring forth as it is read through the centuries.

Following the Bible, the oral tradition developed in several different directions. Ritual and ethical teachings were finally written down around the year 200 CE to form the Mishnah, which then served as the basis for a three-century conversation among teachers that, when added to the text of the Mishnah, became the Talmud around 500 CE. At the same time the Talmud was being developed, stories and legends based on biblical characters and rhythms appeared and were collected in volumes generally titled Midrash. These were the teaching stories of the Rabbis, and they are still being told and still being written. A third major strand of writings form the expanding world of commentary: commentary on the Bible, on the Talmud, and on the Midrash. Jews were the first "People of the Book," but sometimes I think *book* should be plural.

In addition to religious texts, Judaism has a history that flows from ancient times through today and beyond. Although the settling of Jews outside of Palestine (known as the "Diaspora") officially began when the Second Temple was destroyed in 70 CE, Jews had begun to move out into the larger world even earlier. After Palestine, the next center of Jewish life was Babylonia—modern-day Iraq. There, the Babylonian Talmud was compiled and written, and the major teachers of the first five hundred years of the Common Era lived and taught.

From there, centers of Jewish life developed in most areas of the known world. The contact with different cultures affected the evolution of Jewish observance, and a true standardization of Jewish practice is a relatively modern thing, developing with the speed of modern communications. While contemporary Judaism springs from the foundation of the Hebrew Bible and is rooted there, the branches and the leaves have expanded into new flowerings.

Jews do not need to be saved. Every once in a while, I meet Christians who wonder how someone could *not* believe in Jesus. I've seen their shock when I respond that we consider everyone to be a son or daughter of God, but do not believe that there was just one son. Jews do not consider Jesus to be the Messiah. For many Christians, Jews seem to be missing something. And they are often quite willing to point out what is missing and encourage conversion.

Yet I believe that it is possible to know, appreciate, support, and even celebrate with each other without feeling compelled to change our identity. Jews appreciate it when Christians acknowledge that Jews are already complete in their faith, and are not in need of being "saved," or being made whole.

Jews are a socially conscious minority. Most people do not know that Jews comprise less than 2 percent of the population of the United States, that Jews are targeted by hate crimes more often than any other group in America, or that anti-Semitism and anti-Jewish feelings are on the rise again in Europe. This is not an issue involving the Jewish religion, but it is one aspect of the Jewish reality that sometimes makes it seem to others that Jews are defensive and overreact to perceived threats. When we enter into deeper interfaith dialogue, we need to be aware not only of matters of belief but also of some of the sociological realities that are in play.

Jewish sensitivity to minority status as well as the prophetic ideal of justice led to the significant Jewish involvement in the civil rights movement of the twentieth century. There is a deep commitment to social justice springing from Jewish texts and from the Jewish experience itself. From ancient days to the present, the

Torah verse speaks of this focus: "You shall not oppress the stranger, for you know what it is to be a stranger, because you were strangers in the land of Egypt" (Exodus 23:9, JPS).

Sheikh Jamal: What I Find Awkward in Islam

Exclusivity. There's a time-honored story that tells how God, over the ages, reveals certain basic truths to people, but then the devil comes along and says, "Let me organize it for you." This becomes religion! Too often when spiritual teachings become institutionalized, the organized religion then claims superiority over all other faiths and highlights particular verses to support its claim.

It's no different with Islam. Sadly, the Muslim ego, like the ego of any other persuasion, many times insists on its own version of the truth. To such an ego, the Qur'an is the true and unadulterated version of divine revelations sent earlier but corrupted by Jews and Christians. Add to this the verse that says that the Prophet Muhammad is the seal of the Prophets (meaning that there will be no more prophets of revelation until the Day of Judgment), and this exacerbates the attitude that Islam is superior to all other religions.

Certain verses in the Qur'an are insulting and awkward. For example, the Holy Book bestows special praise on the Jews—"I preferred you to all others for My Message" (2:47)—but severely berates the Rabbis for excessive legalism, rationalizing monotheism, and for being trusted with the laws of the Torah but failing to observe them (62:5). Another Qur'anic verse says that the people closest to Muslims in love are Christians, especially the priests and monks (5:82), but roundly criticizes them for saying that "The Lord of Mercy has begotten a son." And the words of disapproval are damning: "God's curse be on them: how they are deluded away from the Truth" (9:30).

Sufi teachers have explained repeatedly that magnifying particular verses that do not support the Universal, and taking them out of context, promotes distortion, illusion, and vanity. The central truth is that the Qur'an emphasizes that each verse has many levels of meaning and "none takes this to heart save those who are endowed with insight" (3:7, trans. Asad).

Sword verses. When Islam took root in the Arabian Peninsula in the seventh century, Islam was a tiny, embryonic movement, struggling to survive, besieged and vastly outnumbered by opposing forces. In that context, the Qur'an gave the community permission to fight but only in self-defense.

Yet the verses most quoted by the Western media and abused by Islamic extremists are the so-called "sword verses" that call for killing the unbelievers: "Slay them wherever you may come upon them, and drive them away from wherever they drove you away" (2:191, trans. Asad). This is a typical example of a verse taken out of context. The verse immediately preceding it warns Muslims not to begin hostilities, "for God loves not the aggressors," and the verse ends with the following injunction: "but if they cease, let there be no hostility ... and know that God is with those who restrain themselves" (2:193–194).

Despite the pre- and post-sword verses, even though the Qur'an comprises over six thousand verses and, of those, only fifty refer to warfare, I have to admit that the sword verses are difficult to explain away. I believe that they need to be understood in a higher light. Besides having a historical context, perhaps these verses are also meant to be metaphors for an inner warfare where God is asking us to overcome the false worshippers of greed and arrogance within ourselves.

Qawwama **and** *daraba.* Despite the revolutionary rights granted to women in the seventh-century Qur'an and the teachings of the Prophet, the position of Muslim women overall today is a distant second class. The sad truth is that the radical Qur'anic privileges of divorce, property, and inheritance rights bestowed on women enraged the men of the tribal culture, and soon after the Prophet's death, male jurists in Arabia and the patriarchal feudal societies used their religious and political authority to reclaim dominance over women.

Perhaps no verse in the Qur'an has caused more hurt to women—physically, emotionally, and mentally—than verse 34 in chapter 4. The meaning and intent of this verse rely on the inter-pretation of two words, *qawwama* and *daraba*. Because Arabic words have multiple meanings, the word *qawwama* implies "ruler" and "manager," but also "protector" and "supporter." The word *daraba* can mean "beat" but also "go along with," "turn away from," and "have consensual sex." Here are two translations of the same text by two male scholars. Note the differences in their versions of *qawwama* and *daraba*:

> Men are the managers of the affairs of women ... as for those women whose defiance you have cause to fear, admonish them and keep them apart from your beds and beat them. (trans. A. A. Maududi)

> Men are the support of women ... as for women you feel are averse, talk to them persuasively, then leave them alone in bed without molesting them and go to bed with them when they are willing. (trans. Ahmed Ali)

Contemporary female Islamic scholars explain that the need to "support" women is in the context of childbearing and that, prop-erly interpreted, the verse does not grant more power to men than to women. Rather, it ensures that when women are in the stages of childbearing and child rearing, they do not have the additional responsibility of earning money. To reinforce the interpretation of *daraba* as "turn away from," the same scholars cite the sayings of the Prophet: "Never beat God's handmaiden" and "It is ignorant men who dominate women." The interpretation of Qur'anic verses by women scholars is bringing depth and balance to our under-

standing of them. It reinforces the insight by sages that we do not
see things as they are; we see things as we are.

Sheikh Jamal: What I Am Grateful for in Islam

The focus on the beauty of our creation. Whenever I despair
about myself and others, I remind myself of the beautiful things
that the Qur'an says about human beings, such as "We have created
[humanity] in the best of molds" (95:4). Instantly, I feel a surge of
joy and hope. My heart fills with gratitude.

In Islamic tradition all humans are *fitra,* meaning essentially
good and noble. In the words of the Holy Book, God fashioned
humanity from water and clay and then "breathed into us" something of the divine Spirit. God even asked the angels to bow to
humanity, and when they hesitated, our Creator explained that the
"names of all things" had been placed uniquely in the hands of
humanity. Indeed, we humans have been created based on the
most beautiful model.

The Islamic belief in the tender caring, affection, and respect
with which God treats us human beings touches me profoundly. If
God wanted, we could have arrived on earth as perfect creatures,
but instead, out of a mysterious and compassionate design, God
created us with free will. At every moment we have a choice. Based
on our decisions, we can sink to "the lowest of the low" or evolve
into beings higher than angels. The potential within humans is
astounding. God wants us to succeed by evolving into the fullness
of our beings. No matter how we flounder about in our dramas and
melodramas, God sustains us.

I am amazed at the definition of *triumph supreme* in the
Qur'an: "Well pleased is God with them and well pleased are they
with God: This is the triumph supreme" (5:119, trans. Asad). And
the words of the Prophet in a well-known *Hadith* are deeply reassuring: "Take one step toward God, and God takes seven steps
toward you; walk to God, and God comes running to you."

The esteem of males and females. In Islamic tradition, God's high esteem of the "children of Adam" extends to males and females alike, a belief that is rooted in the Creation story. The Holy Book mentions not only Adam but also his spouse in the Garden of Eden, and says that it was Satan who beguiled them into making wrong choices. When exiled from the garden, both Adam and his spouse begged forgiveness. The All-Merciful God not only forgave but exalted them by appointing them and their descendants "vice-regents of God on earth." About relations between men and women, a verse of beauty says, "It is [God] who has created you all out of one living entity and out of it brought into being its mate, so that man might incline with love toward woman" (7:189, trans. Asad).

The respect for diversity. Some awkward verses notwithstanding, the Qur'an has an abundance of verses celebrating diversity. One verse says that God could have made all of humanity one single community, but out of a compassionate divine plan, God created a diversity of "tongues and colors" (30:22). Humanity in its diversity is invited into "the Abode of Peace" (10:25, trans. Asad), and we are encouraged to "strive as in a race in all virtues; the goal of you all is to Allah" (5:48). A primary teaching of the Qur'an and of Islamic sages is that God wants us to embrace differences and coexist joyously. No matter what our faith, within each one of us is the Breath of God.

The universal verses about diversity and inclusiveness in the Qur'an are extraordinary. What earns a person entrance to heaven is neither gender nor religion—be they "male or female," "Jew, Christian, or Sabian"—but having faith in God and, more important, doing righteous deeds (4:124 and 5:69). The phrase *righteous deeds* appears repeatedly in the Holy Book. God has created diversity so that we might do the righteous deed of getting to "know one another" (49:13). In a touching verse, it is stated that God wants no more reward for the gift of the Qur'an than for us to love each other (42:23).

Sheikh Jamal: What I Want Others to Know about Islam

The respect for all religions. Many will be surprised to know that the Qur'an is a good guide for interfaith understanding and harmony. Fully one-fourth of the Qur'an is devoted to stories about prophets who came before Muhammad, and Muslims are repeatedly asked not to make any distinction between any of the prophets, including Muhammad. The Holy Book refers to Abraham as "friend of God," to Moses (who is mentioned as often as Muhammad) as "one to whom God spoke," to Jesus as "spirit of God," and to Muhammad as "messenger of God." The Qur'an talks about the virgin birth of Jesus and says that this great prophet was created in the same mold as Adam. Mary, the mother of Jesus, warrants a separate chapter in the Qur'an, which calls her the "holiest of the holy."

God asks us to honor and respect revelations sent to prophets of all religions:

> We believe in God, and in that which has been bestowed from on high upon us, and that which has been bestowed upon Abraham and Ishmael and Isaac and Jacob and their descendants, and that which has been vouchsafed to Moses and Jesus, and that which has been vouchsafed to all the other prophets by their Sustainer: We make no distinction between any of them. And it is unto Him that we surrender ourselves. (2:136, trans. Asad)

The meaning of *jihad.* Ever since 9/11, the word *violence* immediately calls to mind fear of Muslim terrorists. The Western media tend to portray radical Muslims willing to kill each other and all "unbelievers" in the name of jihad. It is crucial to understand that these angry people do not accurately reflect the roots of Islam. Most of them are motivated by a need for political power, a need that stems from a sense of powerlessness and helplessness in their own society. It is also important to appreciate that Muslim radicals make up only a tiny minority of the Islamic population.

In this context it is significant to note that the concept of *jihad* has been abused and misused by Muslims and non-Muslims alike. The word *jihad* literally means "effort" or "exertion." The primary focus in Islam is on the *greater* jihad, which is the struggle to transform the base attributes of oneself, to enrich one's relationships with family, friends, and community, and to bring justice to the world. What non-Muslims perceive as jihad is actually the *lesser* jihad to protect one's self, family, property, and faith *when attacked*. It is critical to note that the concept of jihad as holy war simply does not exist in the Qur'an.

The spirituality of Islam. Spirituality abounds in Islam. The Qur'an is a wellspring of guidance, discernment, remembrance of God, and mercy for seekers of any faith. When explaining discernment, for example, Islamic spiritual teachers ask us to differentiate between the voice of Moses and the pharaoh inside of us. In seeking remembrance of God, Muslims will recite or chant praises in God's name. By praising God, we are creating "feathers" and "wings" for "the bird of Spirit" in us. This metaphor is derived from a Qur'anic story in which Jesus poured his praise of God into birds of clay, whereupon the birds sprouted wings and flew away. To invoke the divine feminine qualities of mercy, nurturance, and tenderness, which are essential if we are to give birth to our true selves, an Islamic teacher will talk of Mary, who, according to the Qur'an, suffered birth pangs as she gave birth to Jesus. Remember, these teachers say, that it takes the receptacle of a Mary to give birth to Jesus, who, in Islamic spirituality, is our higher self. It is always a struggle to give birth to our own higher self. Only in the womb of mercy and tenderness will our true self gestate and emerge.

The nature of Muhammad. A Muslim will never invoke the name of Jesus or a Jewish prophet without immediately saying, "Peace and greetings be upon him." What wounds a Muslim most deeply is when some Christians and Jews revile Muhammad. Most do not know that, from an early age, Muhammad felt a calling to proclaim the Oneness of God or that he was an administrator, a community builder, a mediator, a judge, a treaty maker, a political and military leader, a spiritual leader, and a prophet who miraculously united the warring tribes and laid the groundwork for Islam to become a world civilization. Those who have criticized him for his marriages do not know that for twenty-five years he was married to one woman, his beloved Khadija. The women he married after her death, save for one, he took under his protection because they were slaves, widows, or divorcees who were considered discards in that community.

What is also not commonly known in the West is that Muhammad was a profound mystic who, even as a child, regularly spent considerable time in the mountains of Mecca in meditation and reflection. His two major epiphanies—the Night of Power, when the first verses of the Qur'an descended upon him, and the Night Journey, when he ascended the seven levels of heaven—are the foundations of Islamic spirituality. Muslims delight in contemplating the words of the Prophet as if "they were roses gathered in the skirt of one's robes."

And perhaps one vital piece of information in the understanding of Islam is that the Prophet Muhammad advocated tirelessly for harmonious relations with the "People of the Book." He famously said, "Anyone who wrongs a Jew or a Christian will have me as his accuser on the Day of Judgment."

Living into Deeper Sharing

As the three of us shared these important disclosures about our faith traditions, we became more convinced than ever that our friendship was the foundation that enabled us to trust each other not only with the beautiful aspects of our faiths, but with our discomforts. We felt liberated because we no longer needed to be defensive. Acknowledging the awkwardness, we could more freely reinterpret those particulars in the service of a shared Universal.

We are convinced that many of you already have friendships that can support this kind of stage 3 dialogue. Look at your relationships with those of other faiths and consider if you are ready for this stage. If so, we find it is best to take responsibility when initiating such new conversations, rather than asking questions of another. If you find that you want to engage in a more complete sharing, consider talking first about the ways in which people of different traditions often misunderstand elements of each other's faiths. For example, you might share some of the ways in which you think that your own faith is misunderstood. What do you find awkward in your own tradition? What is it you would most like the other to know about your faith tradition? And then invite your partner in this venture to share from his or her own perspective. This kind of openhearted sharing not only builds on the friendship you have already established, but it can also create a far greater level of communication and a far more expansive understanding of your faith and theirs.

∽

5

PERSPECTIVES ON ISRAEL AND PALESTINE

Moving Beyond Safe Territory

The Elephant in the Room

As we deepen our interfaith dialogue, it is important to ask, "What have we been avoiding? Is there an elephant in the room?" This brings us to stage 4 of the interfaith dialogue: moving beyond "safe territory." This is the critical juncture where we need to face honestly the differences that are fraught with difficulty, the issues for which there are no easy answers. This is the point where relationships provide the greatest opportunity for growth—and the greatest challenges. There's no way around it: growth always involves challenges.

And there is perhaps no greater challenge among Christians, Jews, and Muslims today than the relationship between the State of Israel and the surrounding Arab nations. At the beginning of our relationship, though we did not spend much time talking about Israel and Palestine, we did know that each of us wanted the same thing for Israelis and Palestinians: full access to all human and civil rights and an end to violence. More than that, we sought to support a culture in which people could help each other rather than hurt each other. Yet as our relationship developed, we realized that we could not fully participate in an honest interfaith understanding and not explore this topic further.

Truthfully, our more vigorous disagreements occurred when talking about the Middle East because, even though we share a hope for a positive outcome there, we bring different perspectives and experiences as a Christian, a Jew, and a Muslim. During these discussions we have learned to ask the question "What does it feel like to be the other?" This question has helped us develop a level of empathy that has been key to our ability to engage in issues of emotional intensity. This empathy speaks to the enduring nature of our personal relationship. Beyond politics, even beyond religion, we meet as individuals on a spiritual journey. We are seeking spaces of healing and wholeness, and we each trust that the motives of the other support this search.

As we talked about ways to continue the discussion of the difficult topic of the Middle East, we couldn't think of a better opportunity to share and deepen our spiritual paths than an interfaith spiritual journey to Israel and Palestine. So in the fall of 2005, the three of us led a group of some forty individuals on an exploration of the sacred sites in the Holy Land from which so many of our spiritual teachings emerged. We were a mixed multitude of Christians and Jews. Jamal was the only Muslim (understandably, Israel is not an appealing tourist destination for most Muslims).

While we were there, the trip went better than we might have expected. It was not until we read each other's words in the first drafts of this chapter that we realized that we had some unfinished business and sparks began to fly. Ted revealed that it had been difficult for him to share Jamal's delight as they gazed at the Dome of the Rock: beautiful though it is, it stands on the ruins of the Temple belonging to his own people. The conversation quickly turned to the current conflict between the Israelis and the Palestinians, aka "the Jews" and "the Muslims."

In the ensuing discussion, the silences were at times louder than the words.

We can certainly understand how interfaith groups often agree not to discuss the Middle East, at least not at the beginning, because a level of trust must be developed before such topics can be addressed. Yet, at the same time, people want to talk about it—especially when the three of us are speaking together at workshops and other events. Although it is a difficult topic to confront, we find ourselves grateful to be able to address issues regarding the Middle East. The dynamics of the conflict, with deep feelings of pain leading to the desire for revenge, demonstrate the very need for the work we are doing.

Perhaps the most important thing we learned on our trip is that we must learn to hear each other and know that we will be heard in return. As we share something of our own personal journeys in the land where it all began, we hope you will catch a glimpse of the possibilities of this stage of interfaith growth.

A Christian in Israel and Palestine

From my window seat on the plane, I can see Israel and, looking north, maybe even Lebanon, where my wife, Judy, and I lived beginning in the fall of 1966. When we were evacuated on June 7, 1967, during the Six-Day War, we could not know then that we would not return, nor did we know or yet understand just how traumatic that sudden departure, dodging snipers' bullets twice, would be for us and how that trauma would shape the rest of our lives.

Now it is November 2005, and this is my first time back to the Middle East. The thrill of coming back, of being given the opportunity to address that unfinished business in Lebanon, has me riveted on what I can see out my window. There is a lump in my throat. I am so focused that I am only barely aware that I am sitting up straight and taking deep breaths, trying to take in what I am seeing.

Evening at the eastern shore of the Mediterranean brings up lights from villages and cities, making a scene where it seems that all is well. I see those lights, and I imagine homes where everyone is feeling loved, safe, and secure, homes where families gather for meals, sleep safely in their beds, and greet their neighbors with goodwill and camaraderie. But this is the Middle East, and I know that all is *not* well.

In my heart I want to think that life in Israel and the Middle East as a whole is basically the same as it is throughout the world. People eat, sleep, go to work, long for those relationships that comfort them, and do everything they can to believe that their worth is at least the same as everyone else's. But in Israel there is a reality that weakens all these ordinary scenarios. For Israel aspires to be the safe haven for Jews who have suffered indignities and violence because of the Christian repudiation of Judaism, the conviction that Jews have not seen the true light of Christianity. The anti-Judaism, expressed most dramatically in the Crusades, the Inquisition, and the Holocaust, has resulted in human suffering that cannot be measured, cannot be imagined by Christians, and violates the very essence of the message of Jesus. How could this situation be any worse?

What makes it worse is the hidden reality that somewhere between 450,000 and 750,000 Palestinians were displaced to create the State of Israel. By both Israeli and Palestinian statistics, today that number exceeds 4 million, mostly living in refugee camps on the West Bank and in Lebanon, Syria, Jordan, and the Gaza Strip. The camps exist for two reasons. The instructions from the Arab League in 1948 were to bar Palestinians from citizenship in other Arab countries. Jordan has granted citizenship to all Palestinians actually living in Jordan, and Lebanon has granted citizenship to some Palestinians, but those are the exceptions. The other reason for refugee camps is that they house people for whom taking up citizenship in another country would be a visible admission that they were giving up homes and land that they feel is rightfully theirs. All of this became much worse when, following the Six-Day War, Israel occupied the West Bank and the Gaza Strip.

This is the other lump in my throat as I look out over that evening landscape. How could it possibly be that two oppressed peoples have come to violence against *each other*? As a Christian flying into Tel Aviv, I have to face the reality that the root cause of the conflict has been the actions of the Christian church over the two millennia since the time of Jesus. The power of repudiation, of coercion, of violence has been used by the Christian church to empower itself at the expense of others. What does it mean, I ask myself now, seeing darkness closing in as we make our final approach to Ben Gurion Airport, to be a Christian in Israel and Palestine? I am on this trip seeking answers to that question.

I was traveling with Jamal, Ted having arrived a couple of days earlier. Jamal and I had not taken more than three steps off the jetway when a security guard politely pulled him aside. I stood by, trying to take in the full meaning of the moment. Jamal's birthplace is Bangladesh; his skin is dark, and his look is Islamic. The racial profiling upset me. I wasn't worried about Jamal, the son of a diplomat who has lived all over the world, but I needed to understand more about why this was happening. I was outside the moment, in a place of privilege, experiencing the pathos of both sides of a conflict alongside my concern for my friend and his sense of himself. As a Christian here, I seemed to be witness to, but not part of, a conflict roiling underneath the surface of ordinary life.

Night at the Wailing Wall

After finally clearing customs, we took a bus to Jerusalem and joined the rest of our group. The first stop on our trip was the Western or Wailing Wall, one remnant of the wall around the original Temple in Jerusalem where the Dome of the Rock, an Islamic shrine, now sits. As we approached the entrance to the area, Jamal and I were each given a *kippah*, the skullcap worn by observant Jews. I put it on and approached the Wall with feelings of belonging and not belonging. It was dark, and we were among many Jews praying and rocking back and forth, the men separated from the women. I *was* made to feel welcome, but I am not Jewish, so being a Christian meant that I was not really part of anything going on there—not part of the praying, not part of the tension between Palestinians and Israelis, not part of anything occurring on that sacred landscape.

For me, that night, all the good accomplished by the Christian church was obscured by the reality of the Christian treatment of Jews. As a Christian, I am a spiritual heir to those responsible for such pain and suffering, the Christians who, in the name of Christ and the church, persecuted and murdered Jews and Muslims. Coming into Israel as a Christian brought me pain: pain because of the disconnect between the substance of Jesus's teachings and the behavior of the Christian church over the intervening two thousand years, and pain because of the suffering and unhappiness of so many living in Israel and Palestine. But as a Christian I am also a spiritual heir to some of the strongest teachings concerning forgiveness and reconciliation. I knew that whatever anguish I felt needed to be converted to reconciliation if I were to contribute to hope.

Sadness and Gratitude

As dramatic as the stop at the Wailing Wall was, the next pair of stops made me angry, sad, confused, anxious, and afraid. On Sunday, we visited *Yad Vashem*, the Holocaust memorial near Jerusalem. Later, we visited Bethlehem on the West Bank just a few miles away. Even now, I am still trying to assimilate these two pieces of the journey. As I look back on the trip, I need to begin with my experience in Bethlehem.

To get to Bethlehem, we had to pass through the government-constructed wall, a thirty-foot-high concrete structure with guard towers reminiscent of scenes from concentration camps during World War II. After we got off our bus and walked across the no-man's land to the other side, we boarded another bus and were taken to a Palestinian social service agency, *Wi'am,* which is dedicated to conflict resolution and is headed by a gracious and caring Palestinian named Zoughbi Zoughbi. It was Zoughbi who helped us to understand the situation in Bethlehem: the depression, the high unemployment, and the idleness that is part of the fertile ground for terrorism and suicide bombing, the shrinking tax base—*and* the deep desire for peace and for justice, a desire shared by many, many Israelis.

The graffiti on the Palestinian side of the wall is in English, expressing anger at the Israelis, even comparing them to Nazis. They want Americans to know that they feel a deep sense of rage at the injustices they experience. Zoughbi was able to convey this with dignity and hope, rather than hatred and fear. For me, the day was filled with sadness for the Palestinians and gratitude for Zoughbi's grace and patience and caring.

It's not very far from Zoughbi's agency in Bethlehem to *Yad Vashem,* the Holocaust Martyrs' and Heroes' Remembrance Authority, near Jerusalem. There, the photographs of the Warsaw Ghetto, the uprising in the ghetto, and the deportation to the death camps show the Jewish side of the suffering. And there the suffering is the consequence of actions by Christians, many of whom justified their involvement in the violence by a sense that they were carrying out the will of God. While there was significant official Christian resistance to the policies of the Third Reich, many Germans were members of congregations whose pastors were supportive of Nazism. These two days strengthened my belief that both Israelis and Palestinians deserve a secure place to live. I was also left with questions. What does compensation mean for both sides? What does forgiveness mean for both sides? How can reconciliation be achieved? How can we help? Working toward the answers to these questions with particular reference to Israel and Palestine, but also with reference to any place where religion appears to play a negative role in social or cultural arrangements, is a very important part of deeper interfaith work.

Standing Together

One of my favorite photographs from the trip is a picture of Ted, Jamal, and me, taken by a member of our group. I am standing next to Ted, who is next to Jamal. We are on the porch of the Church of St. Peter Gallicantu, and the Dome of the Rock is visible in the background. There we stood, the three of us—representatives of Judaism, Islam, and Christianity. We are connected, and we are supporting each other. I am close to tears. Here we are at one of the physical centers of the spiritual universe for our three traditions, and instead of standing apart, we are standing together—no, more than together. We are standing, blessed by the sunshine of the moment, with a determination to help turn a sort of historic corner. We know that we can't do this alone, but we are taking a first step, and the depth of the moment ... well, it is too deep for words.

Together (from left) Jamal, Ted, and Don stand on holy ground.
Photo: © 2005 by Don Mackenzie, Ted Falcon and Jamal Rahman.

As I write about this three years later, I am sitting by the fire in our living room in Seattle. The Christmas tree lights are on, and as the day dawns, I can see Lake Washington and the homes across the lake with their lights coming on, reminding me of what I had seen from the plane as we were nearing Tel Aviv. The lights suggest security and comfort, something I am feeling right now. At the same time, I am thinking of the people who live in Israel and in Palestine. In Israel, there is fear. Many people are armed, and security is a major concern, as it has been for Jews since well before the time of Jesus. In Bethlehem and in other parts of the West Bank and the Gaza Strip, there is depression, extremely high unemployment (60 percent and higher), and an air of hopelessness, imprisonment, and anger. I can see both groups in my mind and hold each in my prayers.

Recently, Judy and I saw a film titled *Then She Found Me*, a film partially about adoption. Since both our children are adopted from Korea, we were very interested in it. At one point, the adopted sibling in the family says to the other, "You don't know what it feels like to be adopted." The other, nonadopted sibling replies, "You don't know what it feels like to be *not* adopted." Often, we assume that we know what it feels like to be the "other," and we may assume that the other doesn't really understand us. Neither of these conditions is ever fully true or fully false. But by listening carefully, we can get closer to the truth of what the other is feeling, thinking, and experiencing. Within that attempt lies the hope that reconciliation and justice can be achieved with deeper understanding, compassion, collaboration, and forgiveness.

The conflict between the Israelis and the Palestinians is not about the differences between Judaism and Islam. It is about politics and culture disguised as religion. It is about a European sensibility colliding with a Middle Eastern sensibility. It is about the tension among wealth, poverty, and humiliation. It is about the suffering of Jews at the hands of Christians (and to a much lesser extent at the hands of Muslims) throughout the centuries. It is about the suffering of Arabs at the hands of the colonial powers—

England and France at the 1919 Treaty of Versailles—which, at the time, was the end of self-government for most Arabs.

Both sides want and deserve respect. Both sides deserve safety, security, and peace, in particular. Both sides need hope— hope that there is a better world coming, hope for a life where the image that came to me flying into Tel Aviv would be more reality than fantasy.

But there is a sense of imprisonment that keeps each side from hearing the other. For Palestinians, it is the reality of displacement. For Israel it is the deep and very important need for safety and security. My hope is that the love at the core of Jesus's teachings will contribute to making real the oneness that arises in Judaism and the compassion so central to Islam. The universals of love and all the things that come from love—cooperation, compassion, for-giveness, reconciliation, and justice—unite us. The challenge is to remain true to these shared universals. For me, that love became real as I stood between Ted and Jamal overlooking Jerusalem.

A Jew in Israel and Palestine

I love Israel. I think it's in my blood. Certainly it's in my name, given to me in honor of Theodor Herzl (1860–1904), the father of modern political Zionism, the movement that resulted in the estab-lishment of the State of Israel in 1948. All the same, I have very mixed feelings when I visit Israel.

This trip with Pastor Don and Sheikh Jamal was not my first trip to Israel. In the spring of 1970, I went with members of my first congregation and attended sessions of the first Jerusalem meeting of the Central Conference of American Rabbis. I remem-ber the first hours most clearly.

We were met at the airport by the tour bus that carried us to Jerusalem. On the way, the guide was talking about pilgrimage and the return to Israel that brought new life to so many Jews since the late 1940s. I thought, a little cynically, "I wonder how many times he's repeated this talk." And suddenly tears ran down my cheeks. I do not cry easily, yet my throat had tightened, and I was weeping. Entering Jerusalem that first time, I was deeply moved.

I don't know if a non-Jew, or even many younger Jews, can fully understand what Israel represented for me. On an ancient level, Israel is the Place of our People. Abraham, Isaac, Jacob, Sarah, Rebecca, Leah, and Rachel all walked here and became part of the foundation of my faith. My people, beginning with an ancient wandering, created a kingdom here centuries later. When the early kingdoms crumbled and we were forced to leave, we knew we were in exile. Psalmists and prophets reminded us of our sacred connection to this land. Much later, exiled once again toward the end of the first century CE, our traditional daily prayers emphasized the central importance of Israel no matter how distant it appeared. Jews endured through their connection to this place, and that connection continued through prayer, study, memory, and yearning for many centuries.

Even with that sense of exile, we sought to create our homes elsewhere and gradually felt the sharpness of our displacement easing. Nowhere were we as much "at home" as in early twentieth-century Germany. There we Jews were integral parts of the nation's culture and commerce. We were scientists, teachers, musicians, artists, physicians, and even government leaders. Germany's Jews mostly considered themselves proudly German—fully assimilated into the surrounding cultural life. So it is a small wonder that so many German Jews failed to appreciate the threat of the Nazi anti-Jewish movement. The shift that spelled their destruction under the leadership of Hitler was for too long perceived to be simply "impossible."

When Israel was established in 1948 as a homeland where Jews everywhere could always find refuge, an ancient dream dovetailed with a modern need. Country after country had turned back boatloads of Jews fleeing Germany. It appeared that no one really cared. Even the United States, where Jews had already created a major presence, provided little help for the millions who were brutalized and killed by the Nazis.

I am not a supporter of Israel's leaders when they do not support the creation of a viable Palestinian state. But no matter how much I might criticize, no matter how strongly I argue for the rights of both Israelis and Palestinians, there is no doubt that I hold the existence of the State of Israel as a Jewish place of sanctuary to be essential. I don't know if non-Jews can understand this apparent dichotomy. To the extent that they can, they are able to appreciate more fully the significance of the secure existence of Israel for most Jews, even though we may never ourselves live there.

So perhaps I should not have been surprised when I wept on that first drive into Jerusalem. At that moment, Israel was real for me. In some sense, it was home.

But Is the Rabbi a Rabbi in Israel?

As much as I felt I had come home, I also realized that I am not the rabbi in Israel that I am anywhere else. As a Reform rabbi, I am marginalized in Israel, where the Orthodox rabbinate has the authority to make the rules, and only Orthodox rabbis can perform many rabbinic functions. Although Reform and Conservative Judaism now have congregations in Israel, only Orthodox rabbis are able to perform marriages and conversions. The majority of the Orthodox establishment is not open to non-Orthodox expressions of the Jewish faith.

So this was one of the differences among my Christian and Muslim colleagues and me as we toured Israel. Don was as much a Christian minister in Israel as he is in the United States, and Jamal as much a Sufi Muslim teacher. Yet as a Jew in my homeland, paradoxically, I did not feel at home religiously. But I did feel a deep connection to the land, so I was eager to have Jamal and Don meet the Israel that I love. Any anxieties I might have had about their comfort in Israel disappeared as we all responded to the spiritual richness of the land we traveled.

It was particularly thrilling to introduce them to the history that comes alive in Jerusalem, to the natural beauty of the Galilee in the north, and to the deep silences of the desert regions in the south. For such a tiny country, Israel includes amazingly diverse landscapes. At its longest point, the country is 260 miles long; at its widest point it is just 60 miles wide, and at its narrowest, 3 to 6 miles wide. It is roughly the size of New Jersey. Yet what Israel contains is a spiritual past and a spiritual present—it encourages a spiritual quest that touches each of our faiths deeply.

What about Palestine?

When we journeyed to Bethlehem, to the south of Jerusalem on the West Bank, it seemed as if we had entered an entirely different country. Our Israeli tour bus stopped outside the gate in the wall—a section of the over 400-mile-long barrier made up of cement walls, fencing, and barbed wire. The wall is an ugly and forbidding structure, meant to increase Israel's security but clearly inhibiting the freedom of those on the other side.

We were to walk through the gate and find a Palestinian tour bus on the other side. What sounded simple became a tension-filled time. We could see no bus. Instead, on the other side of the wall, graffiti attacked Israel in no uncertain terms. An atmosphere of anger surrounded a few young men who were hanging around near the gate. Perhaps some of the fear springing up within me reflected feelings of those who lived with that wall as part of their everyday lives.

After what seemed like the longest walk on our trip, we found the bus and pretended that everything was just fine. We went to meet with a Palestinian named Zoughbi Zoughbi, who was very hospitable and spoke of his Peace School for Palestinians, and his hopes for a brighter and more peaceful future for all in the area.

I confess to a feeling of relief when we returned to the other side of that wall. There is no doubt that the Palestinians there are living in greater poverty than we witnessed elsewhere in Israel, and the wall further constrains their ability to attract tourist dollars. That the Palestinians need their own autonomy, their own state, and their own freedom was clear to us. We all wished the way to achieve that peacefully were clearer.

The suffering and the fear on both sides are palpable and real. We know that the fear and suffering need to be acknowledged, need to be heard, and need to be addressed. It was important for us to be there, to witness, that we might speak more clearly a message of hope and possibility.

Is This Appropriate for a Rabbi?

On this interfaith trip we visited more Christian sites than I had ever seen before. I learned that wherever something important happened in the story of Jesus, a church was later built. Some are ancient, some modern; some ostentatious, some more simple—all kinds of churches.

The Church of the Holy Sepulchre in Jerusalem is among the most impressive as well as the most confusing. Descendants of two prominent Palestinian Muslim families hold the key to the building. The saladin of the Ottoman Empire began that arrangement some eight hundred years ago, in an effort to avoid conflicts among the six Christian sects that inhabit different chapels, halls, and corridors of the vast structure. The current key holder, Wajih Nusseibeh, inherited the post from his father and will hand the key to his son in turn. Mr. Nusseibeh, a proud and rather joyful man who seemed quite happy to have his picture taken with us, greeted our group enthusiastically. One wonders how many pictures he has appeared in. Clearly, he feels very good about welcoming visitors to the church and chatting with them.

Built in the fourth century by order of Emperor Constantine, the Church of the Holy Sepulchre marks the "official" site of the crucifixion, burial, and resurrection of Jesus. (Another site, called the Garden Tomb, is just outside the walls of the old city and is also claimed to be the setting of these events.) From the outside, the church is hemmed in by numerous other buildings and churches that have accumulated over the centuries. Inside, it appears cavernous and almost Balkanized into separate provinces, symbolized perhaps most clearly by a large closet-sized room standing in the middle of the larger space. One of the monks of the Armenian church always sits inside, laying claim to that sacred space.

There were many tourists on the day we were there, and they were guided to the various sections representing different segments of the Christian church. There was a little line leading to a low wall. People pretty much needed to kneel in order to reach a hand under the wall and down a hole in the floor. The guide said that we could feel the top of the hill through that opening. I found myself vaguely uneasy about getting into line for that attraction, as some part of my consciousness murmured questions about how appropriate this was for a rabbi. When it came my turn, I knelt and sort of crawled into the tiny space and reached my hand through the hole. The ground I touched was far smoother than I had anticipated. I wondered if it had been smoothed over by the millions of hands that must have rubbed against it in the last fifteen hundred years.

What I was touching is believed to be the ground of Calvary, the hill on which the crucifixion took place.

I realized that this church marks the central and defining event of Christianity—the event without which there would be no Christianity. The church sanctifies that place but also hides it from sight. We had no sense of being on a hill; rather, we were in a large and ancient building in the middle of a crowded city. We could touch the hill through a small opening in the floor, but that was as close as we could get to the ground on which this important moment is believed to have taken place.

That image has stayed with me and provided one of the major lessons from this journey: how easy it is for the religious institution to unwittingly obscure the essence of faith.

Tensions Between Form and Essence

What struck me in the Church of the Holy Sepulchre was the difference between an actual experience and the institutionalization of that experience; between spiritual awakening and the religious institutions that are meant to support it.

If you think about it, all religious traditions began in order to support us in our search for the experience of being most alive and most present to our lives. The Abrahamic faiths each reinforce a stronger connection with a Greater Presence. The realization of that Presence conveys a sense of greater oneness, and inspires spiritual seekers to pursue lives of greater intention, love, and compassion. But as our religious institutions evolve, they may become focused on their own survival and their own expansion, and their initial purpose may become more a matter of words spoken and read than lives inspired and lived.

This difficulty is not unique to religious institutions, of course; it is in the nature of all human institutions. Just as the Church of the Holy Sepulchre covered up the very ground of history it was there to honor, so too, all of our institutions tend to hide that which they were created to celebrate. Our countries are institutions of a grand order, yet increasingly their expressed ideals and goals do not actually touch many who are yearning for the nourishment of those ideals and goals. Our social service agencies, while serving many, wind up competing with each other rather than joining together to serve our common need. Our religious institutions tend to fight about the particularities of correct form rather than living the essential love, compassion, and oneness at the heart of their very own spiritual teachings.

This tension between form and essence, in which an institutional structure obscures what it was created to serve, reaches into all our relationships. Too many of us confuse the form with the essence, declaring which relationships are "right" rather than supporting all relationships that are loving and compassionate.

Moments of real connection and personal commitment that defined the beginning of relationships may lead to structures and roles that become institutionalized and very difficult to evolve. We often wind up protecting the form rather than pursuing the essence of our closest relationships.

What if we could find ways to remember what is most important? What if, instead of hiding from each other, we could remember our connection to each other? What if we could reawaken to the true teachings of our faiths behind the establishment of our religious institutions? Wouldn't that empower a spiritual coming-of-age that would spark a cultural evolution?

This, of course, is the work that the three of us have chosen to pursue together. We are striving to celebrate the universal teachings within each of our traditions. In order to do that, we need to hold our institutions as lightly as possible. It's an amazing challenge, at least as difficult in our day as it was so long ago. Yet, perhaps because of the depth of those teachings, all of us carry greater responsibilities for the world in which we live.

Traveling with other faith leaders on this interfaith pilgrimage not only allowed me to see Israel through new eyes, but also allowed me to see myself differently. I realized that I was not defined by external authority. There was no question about it: I *was* a rabbi in Israel. And I saw the three of us in a new light. The land had brought forth profound teachings from all three of our traditions, yet at each of the sites we visited, the message was the same: we are spiritual beings charged with walking that spiritual awareness into our world. We are called to remember the One we are, and to witness that One through each other, always.

A Muslim in Israel and Palestine

When we decided to co-lead an interfaith group to Israel and Palestine, I experienced both excitement and trepidation: excitement because Jerusalem is the site of the Dome of the Rock, the

third holiest place on earth for Muslims, and trepidation because
of the mutual animosity between Israel and the Muslim world.

Every Muslim child grows up hearing about the *miraj*, the
Prophet Muhammad's mystical Night Journey into the upper
realms of Paradise. Rapt in prayer and meditation one evening, the
Prophet was astounded to find himself magically transported from
Mecca to a rocky hilltop in faraway Jerusalem. There, accompanied by the angel Gabriel, he began to ascend seven levels of
heaven. All around him the Prophet beheld luminous angels pros-
trating themselves to God in praise and gratitude. To mark the site
of this glorious journey, the first Muslim caliph, Abu Bakr, the
political leader following the death of the Prophet Muhammad,
built a magnificent mosque capped with a golden dome. I had been
fortunate enough to visit the sacred sites of Mecca and Medina several times in my youth, but the Dome of the Rock had always been
beyond my reach. Now I would be able to complete the treasured
trio of Muslim pilgrimage sites, and I was thrilled at the possibility.

On the other hand, every Muslim child also grows up hearing
about the adversarial nature of the modern State of Israel. In many
Muslim minds, Israel is a massive military machine built in collaboration and collusion with the United States to dominate the
Middle East and, specifically, to deny statehood for the Palestinians.
Having spent some of my formative years in several Middle Eastern
countries, I am very conversant with the politics and struggles of
the leaders and peoples of the region. I have an abiding empathy,
both heartfelt and visceral, for the Palestinian cause. For most
Muslims, Israel's occupation of Palestinian lands and suppression
of the Palestinians' rights is a symbol and a stark reminder of
Islamic hopelessness and helplessness in the modern world.

As a child traveling with my parents, I noticed that my diplo-
matic passport granted me the right to travel to "all countries of
the world except South Africa and Israel." So it felt somewhat
strange, all these years later, to present my American passport and
board a plane for the forbidden land of Israel. I felt curiously

lonely, even though I was flying with good friends and would be supported in Israel by the affection and good wishes of forty-four fellow travelers—some of whom even include Islamic practices in their spiritual lives. Still, I was the only avowed Muslim in our interfaith group. None of my Muslim friends were interested in making the trip. As one of them remarked wryly, "Israel is not exactly a vacation spot for Muslims, you know."

The minute I deplaned at Ben Gurion Airport in Tel Aviv, a security officer approached, asked to see my passport, and began to question me. After repeating the same questions several times and getting the same answers, he noticed that my friends were getting anxious—and perhaps also noticed that one was wearing a Star of David identifying her as a Jew—and finally allowed me to move forward to passport control. There, a young woman punched my name into the computer, gazed at it for some time, and then asked, "What is your religion?" "Islam," I replied. Immediately she asked the people behind me to shift to another line. My case demanded more scrutiny and time.

The woman at passport control asked pointed questions about the purpose of my trip, and for that I was prepared. I handed her a ream of papers, including a flyer advertising the interfaith spiritual journey to the Holy Land co-led by a rabbi, a pastor, and a Muslim cleric. Her eyes settled on the flyer and suddenly her face lit up. Her entire demeanor changed. In an animated, friendly voice, she declared, "Interfaith! Jew, Christian, Muslim, all together! This is good! Very good!"

She picked up the phone, talked to someone, and asked me to follow her. Clutching my passport and papers in one hand, she again emphasized that interfaith was very good. We walked over to her supervisor's office, and as I pressed forward to accompany her inside the office, she beckoned me to sit down in an empty chair and assured me, "Don't worry, I take care of this." In less than five minutes she came out of the office, still beaming. She returned my passport duly stamped, escorted me to customs, and on parting repeated the peace mantra, "Interfaith! This is good! Very good!"

In that moment those sweet, reassuring, hopeful words about interfaith work felt sacred. I felt as though my commitment to interfaith work was divinely validated by the enthusiastic support of this young woman in Israel. For a moment I dared to envision that there was peace between Israel and Palestine—that Jews, Christians, and Muslims were living in peace and friendship. I felt a surge of joy and excitement, and remarkable possibilities unfurled in my mind. Not only would the dynamics of the entire Middle East be transformed, but there would be a global shift in thinking and ways of being!

The next morning those beautiful thoughts and feelings continued to glow in my heart, like embers of a fire, as I stepped onto the balcony of the Church of St. Peter Gallicantu with my Christian and Jewish brothers, Don and Ted. Before us was a panoramic view of the Dome of the Rock rising above the holy city of Jerusalem. The first glimpse of the dazzling golden dome against the brilliant blue sky moved me to the depths of my being.

Standing atop the hill, I experienced a profound initiation, a fresh commitment to surrender my life to God in peace and joy. Something clicked and I felt a divine imprint. In my heart I knew that this was not a fleeting thought that would fade with the passage of time. The Qur'an says repeatedly, "Be conscious of God," and throughout my sojourn in the Holy Land, this insight was uppermost in my mind. Every site we visited deepened my understanding of what it meant to be conscious of God.

Be Conscious of God

My actual visit to the Dome of the Rock ended up being a bittersweet experience. Accompanied by a score of friends who shared my excitement of the moment, I ascended to the imposing square above the city and stood in the shadow of the monument. There I had to leave my friends and go alone, with a Muslim guide, into that sacred space. We all knew our parting was inevitable because the Palestinian guardians of the hilltop, smarting under Israeli rule of the city, exercise the only control they can: they currently ban all non-Muslims from the inside of the Dome of the Rock. The Dome has become a political flashpoint, no longer a place of pure worship.

Saddened by the situation, I nevertheless was profoundly moved by the sight of ordinary men and women praying by the rock inside the mosque from which the Prophet began his ascent into heaven. For the moment, there was nothing political in the hearts of these true Muslims. Their gaze was turned inward and their faces were infused with exquisite sweetness. The rock was perfumed by the fragrance of their devotions.

The Qur'an says that everywhere we turn is the Face of Allah (2:115). Indeed, everywhere I turned in that Holy Land, I saw the Face of Allah in the faces of awe-filled Jews, Christians, and Muslims. Faithful worshippers in places that were holy to Christians and Jews seemed far beyond politics. In the Christian sites where Jesus walked, prayed, agonized, and died, what moved me were the faces of the worshippers. Because of their love for Christ, their faces were alight with love, devotion, and awe. It was the glow on their faces that made the places sacred. At the Wailing Wall, as I watched worshippers sway and bob their heads, reciting and praying, I imagined their offerings climbing the Wall and ascending into the mysterious realms of heaven. But what struck me most was the intensity of the devotees, rapt in humility and vibrant with veneration.

Lost in such musings, I was suddenly aroused by what many a visitor to the Holy Land has felt as a peak experience. Over the murmur of Jewish prayers at the Wall, I began to hear from minarets all around me a most familiar sound: the Muslim call to prayer. And then the church bells began to toll. All at the same time! Such a blending of sounds was the music of the spheres on earth. My heart rang with Rumi's words that what is praised is One, so the praise is one, too. All these religions, all this singing, are really one song!

A quite different experience, not of oneness but of tragic separation, greeted me at *Yad Vashem*, the memorial to the victims of the genocide of European Jewry during World War II. The pictures and stories of cruelty and violence are simply overwhelming. As we toured the many different installations at *Yad Vashem*, our group seemed to walk around in a daze, faces drawn and tearful. At the end of the tour, I sat down alone in silence to commune with my own thoughts and feelings. In that space I could feel true empathy for the Jews in Israel. Certainly it is only humane and just that they have a homeland with a Jewish identity. After all, there are more than fifty Muslim countries with Muslim majorities.

A day later, a few miles south of Jerusalem, we encountered the controversial concrete wall being built by the Israeli government. On the other side of the wall is the gloomy Arab town of Bethlehem. The difference between the Wailing Wall and this political wall is stark and immediate. One is a symbol of sacredness and dignity; the other, of sterility and separation. One exudes sincerity and piety; the other reeks of anger, pain, and suffering. Standing with our group on the Arab side of the wall, listening to the eerie silence and reading messages of anger, hate, and anguish scrawled on the wall, I began to feel a familiar resentment against the high-handed policies of the Israeli government. If the concrete wall is meant to stem the flow of suicide bombers, it also chokes the weak Palestinian economy and arbitrarily and unilaterally defines the border.

Studying the wall, I was reminded of a thirteenth-century story in which the sultan of Konya was proudly showing Rumi's father, Sheikh Burhanuddin, the impressive walls and fortification he had built to keep out invaders. "Yes," said Rumi's father, "this will keep out the invaders, but what will you do about the cries of the oppressed and repressed that can leap a thousand walls?"

Later that evening I saw a Palestinian family in a car at the checkpoint by the wall, returning to Israel. Before the Israeli soldier allowed the car through, he shouted some questions to the driver of the car. From my vantage point I could hear his loud voice. Throughout this exchange, the soldier had a gun pointed not more than six inches from the driver's face. In the darkness I could see the outline of a woman and two children. My heart clenched, and I could feel their humiliation. What would it be like, I wondered silently, to live under these conditions all my life?

It struck me that to be conscious of God when we are wronged is a most difficult undertaking. It means that we must imbue our words and actions with God-consciousness even in the most arduous of circumstances. If we are truly seeking the Face of Allah, we must, as the Qur'an says clearly, "never let hatred of anyone lead you into the sin of deviating from justice. Be just; this is closest to being God-conscious" (5:8, trans. Asad).

In God's Own Sanctuary

The place on the trip where I found the deepest satisfaction was, surprisingly, in the natural setting of Kibbutz Ein Gedi. As soon as we drove into the kibbutz, I knew I was entering a sacred sanctuary. I felt nurtured and nourished by the luscious greenery of the grass and trees, the colors of the flowers, the grandeur of the mountains, the sweet chirping of the birds, and the soothing balm of the ever-flowing breeze. What a joyous relief it was to find that there were no structures called mosque, church, or synagogue here!

Gazing at the open arms of the date palm trees as they gestured heavenward at Ein Gedi, I heard the voice of nature begging me to receive the truth with an open heart. It struck me that, despite the beautiful teachings and injunctions in each of our holy books, we tend to speak and act on our truth of convenience. The natural beauty of blossoms in the botanical gardens reminded me of the human-made beauty of the Dome of the Rock, but now I was aware of the truth that this magnificent edifice is built on the ruins of the ancient Jewish Temple, a source of pain to the Jewish world.

The Qur'an says, "It is not their eyes that are blind but their hearts" (22:46). In the Holy Land, the trials and tribulations of history and politics that have descended on Israelis and Palestinians have closed many hearts. What will open those hearts? The use of force only causes the heart to clench more tightly against the pain. Reason alone will not seduce the heart to open. The only key to a locked heart is forged of qualities that the heart recognizes and trusts as its own: compassion, love, forgiveness, and higher understanding.

There in the sanctuary of Ein Gedi, my heart was able to relax in the knowledge that hundreds of ordinary people are doing the heart work of tearing down walls and nourishing our common humanity. Heartbroken parents of Jewish children killed by Palestinian suicide bombers and of Muslim children killed by Israeli defense forces are reaching out to one another and working to end senseless violence. Individuals on both sides of the wall are transcending the disappointment of circumstances and organizing and collaborating for the cause of peace and mutual well-being. Rabbis and sheikhs, awakening to the heart of their traditions, are daring to speak out about injustices and offering solutions based on compassion and hope. Youth from both sides delight in learning and playing together. These grassroots movements of unsung heroes and heroines who strive to make heart-to-heart connections with the other are, for me, a source of undying hope, joy, and inspiration.

Two Teachings

Back home in the United States, I am often asked to share teachings from my trip.

About walls, occupation, and terrorism, I continue to speak out, but I now have an inner understanding that the conditions in the Holy Land are a reflection of what exists in our own hearts. The Qur'an says that God will not change the condition of a people unless they change what is in their hearts (13:11). This need to change is not limited to hearts in the Holy Land, but includes hearts in all lands where people rant and pass judgments about the situation in the Middle East.

For me, the real question is this: If being just is closest to God-consciousness, am I just with those in my own "holy land"—with my family, friends, and acquaintances? Through words and silence, action and inaction, what walls am I creating in my own life? What little acts of "occupation" and "terror" do I engage in within my own circle? My trip to Israel has made me more mindful of these inner truths.

I have taken to heart an insight derived from a question about the Prophet's Night Journey. Why didn't he ascend to heaven directly from Mecca? Why did he first have to travel to Jerusalem? Some Muslim mystics explain that God is conveying a message to the People of the Book, that to experience heaven on earth we have to first unite Muslims (Mecca) with Jews (Jerusalem).

The sweet words of the young woman in the airport sanctified my interfaith work as "very good." The insight from the Night Journey of the Prophet has sanctified my friendship and collaboration with Ted and Don as essential and sacred.

Blessings at the Galilee

Our interfaith journey to Israel and Palestine was filled with moments of wonder. As the trip entered its final days, Rabbi Ted, who often serves to focus the teaching, realized that he didn't have a clue about the climax needed for the conclusion of the trip. But, sometimes, such a moment simply has to reveal itself in its own time. It happened that way at the Sea of Galilee.

Our group wound up on the shore of the Sea of Galilee, a freshwater lake also called Lake Kinneret or Lake Tiberias. Each of us had planned to give a teaching that afternoon as the group sat on rocks near the water. As often is the case, Rabbi Ted led off and was followed by Pastor Don and then Sheikh Jamal. As Don was talking, Ted was listening and looking at the water. When Don finished, Ted drew him aside, suddenly excited.

"How about baptizing everyone?" Ted asked.

By the time Jamal had finished his teaching, a plan to offer everyone a blessing with water from each of the three traditions was emerging. We were sitting by a body of water that our ancestors had visited. Although much had changed over the centuries, over the millennia, it was probably scientifically true that some elements of the water were the same. To touch that water with sacred intent could, in fact, allow us to connect more fully to the past we each treasured, to the paths we celebrated.

Rabbi Ted knew that his own involvement would be a symbolic *mikveh*, the cleansing bath still practiced by observant Jews that later became baptism in the Christian church. Pastor Don's would be a symbolic baptism. Sheikh Jamal, upon hearing this, realized that he could offer the Muslim *wudu*, the ritual washing before prayer.

So there we were, spread out on the shore, encouraging participants to form three lines. Folks were invited to engage in any or all of the rituals. Rabbi Ted had removed his sandals and waded out into the water. The sharpness of the stones beneath his feet helped keep him focused as he invited those who waded out with him to share the blessing for *mikveh*, attaching the act to holy purpose—a cleansing of the dust that inhibits our awareness of the One we share. Pastor Don invited Christians to reaffirm their baptism in the waters of the Galilee. For those who were not Christian, he offered a baptism blessing, confirming their own spiritual identity. Sheikh Jamal explained to Jews and Christians the sacredness of water in the Qur'an—"We have made from water every living thing" (21:30)—and invited them to join him in prayerfully cleansing the hands, forearms, mouth, nostrils, ears, back of neck, head, face, and feet in a ritual honoring the gift of water to revitalize the spirit and wash away the grime of the world.

There on the shore of the Galilee, people entered the very same water to taste the spiritual richness of the three Abrahamic traditions. It was a time of great clarity and connection. It was the climax of our trip; we were able to honor depths of each other's faiths while standing firmly within our own. We were beginning to know from the inside more about the richness another Way taught, and the spiritual gifts of that moment continue to carry blessing for all of us who were there.

Expanding Our View

As the three of us walked that ancient land, we were profoundly aware of the promise made to our ancestor, Abraham: "I will indeed bless you, and I will make your offspring as numerous as the stars of heaven and as the sand that is on the seashore" (Genesis 22:17, JPS). We understood viscerally that all of us—Jews, Christians, and Muslims—are expressions of and heirs to that promise, and as we shared our journey, we drew closer to the fulfillment of our profoundly spiritual quest.

For the three of us, the trip to Israel and Palestine brought us deeply into stage 4 of the interfaith dialogue: moving beyond safe territory. It not only stimulated our pain and sense of injustice, but it also brought gratitude that we have been granted the blessings of patience and trust. The trip expanded our view and brought us to a new level of sharing and understanding.

While we might wish we could offer the details of a totally just solution—one state or two, with workable borders and compromises—we cannot. Only those living there can develop and bring that vision to fruition. What we can suggest are steps on a path to a place where the solution can make itself known. We believe two things need to happen—both in terms of the sociopolitical situation in Israel and Palestine, and in terms of embracing this fourth stage of interfaith work.

As a first step toward healing, each of us needs to name and share our truths. And that starts on a personal level. Jamal, for his part, needed his rabbi friend, Jews in general, and the world at large, to see and acknowledge the plight of the stateless Palestinians. Ted, who is appalled at the wall and the policies behind it, nevertheless needed the world at large, and his Muslim friend in particular, to acknowledge that Israel's need to defend itself is not gratuitous, is not happening in a vacuum. From the very beginning of its statehood, Israel was under attack by the surrounding Arab countries, who, even now, do not show Israel on the maps of the Middle East used in all their schools and universities. Don, as the middle child in this family of Abraham, in typical middle-child fashion, tried to keep the peace. He often takes responsibility for the quarrel between his Muslim and Jewish cousins by placing the blame on the church's sorry history vis-à-vis Judaism and Islam, yet this particular tension is not the fault of Christianity per se. The anti-Jewish, anti-Islamic attitudes and actions of the church are not the essence of Christianity; in fact, they are the very antithesis of Jesus's life and teaching.

In addition to our individual truths, each of us needs to name the truths of our differing cultures and peoples. A Jewish Israel needs assurance of safety and security. The open wound of Palestinian displacement in 1948 needs to be acknowledged. The loss of hope that contributes to violence needs to be named as well. The positive truths also need to be acknowledged. As much as there is hopelessness, there are also precious resources in each of our faiths that support cooperation, compassion, and forgiveness.

Once our truths are no longer hidden, we have the greatest opportunity for growth. We are ready to take the second step toward healing: Both sides must offer and seek forgiveness. Both sides must offer apologies. Reconciliation is the only path to real peace.

Some may say that our understanding is naive. We would say that the greater naiveté is the belief that problems have ever really been solved through suspicion, hate, and violence. When we demonize the other, there is little chance for meaningful dialogue. No amount of violence can guarantee safety for either side in that conflict. Safety awaits the greater expression of compassion and forgiveness that alone will allow a mutuality of support for peace.

You have probably noticed that problems are never really solved at the level of the problem. That's because these problems arise from our personal biases, fears, and desires for revenge. When we awaken to our shared humanity, we can appreciate that we all share the same basic concerns. As you engage in your own deeper conversations with those of other faiths or convictions, keep in mind the difference between the problem and the essential being of the people involved. This leads to greater hope not only for personal conflicts, but for national and international ones as well. This is the hope at this fourth stage of interfaith work: to move beyond the "safe" topics to openly face the incompatibilities of our different perceptions and to honor each other as full human beings. This is the ground on which true healing between us can be born.

When you face differences with people of other faiths that present challenges to both of you, and your emotions intensify, remember to ask yourself this key question: "What does it feel like to be the other?" Remember that you are each on a spiritual journey, and that this juncture of difficult questions is an opportunity for healing and growth.

🐚

6

NEW DIMENSIONS
OF SPIRITUAL
IDENTITY

Exploring Spiritual Practices from
Other Traditions

A Deeper Taste

We three have a friend who is passionate about Chinese tea. He orders all his tea directly from China; his home is filled with hundreds of different teapots; he describes the various tea leaves with great excitement and appreciation. And over the years, we have sampled the different teas and learned to understand and enjoy the scents and flavors he has shared. Similarly, as the three of us have been involved in spiritual teachings and spiritual practices based in our different faith traditions, as we have taught together at retreats and workshops and shared at each other's worship services and celebrations, and as we have engaged in an evolving process of spiritual direction, we have learned much about each other's spiritual practices and have enjoyed many moments of tasting those practices.

This is stage 5 of the interfaith dialogue: exploring spiritual practices from other traditions. It is a stage of intentional experimentation with practices from each other's faiths and, in one sense, is quite distinct from the previous stages of sharing stories and beliefs— even of confronting differences. As important as these stages are, they still tend to focus on "This is *me* here—what I believe, what my experiences are—and *you* there." In this fifth stage, there is more of a willingness to cross the boundaries, to step into the other's shoes and try out what it is like to be *there*. It's not a stage of shedding your faith but of adding another dimension to your identity. It's a way of experiencing new spiritual practices that reflect the wisdom, the compassion, and the clarity of the ground of another's faith.

For the three of us, deepening our spirituality through experiencing these spiritual practices has profoundly supported our individual journeys. We have learned to trust that the words, the melodies and movements, and the meditations of another's Way can help us experience flavors of spirituality that enhance us all.

In these pages of sharing the development of our relationship with you, it is important to us that we include specific practices that we have experienced together. We invite you to read about our practices and also to experience them. In this way, you will be able to taste a little more deeply the fruits that we have shared in our relationship.

Pastor Don's Practices

The development of Christian spiritual practices is essential to a deeper understanding and experience of Christianity. Practices have been an important part of the Christian experience since the very beginning and can be seen in the life of Jesus when he went off by himself to pray.

Here are some of the practices that I use to help keep myself centered and to be more mindful of my relationship to God and to other people.

Sabbath Moments

Sabbath is a reality that arises from a need for us to stay centered, focused, and able to learn, to grow. It recognizes the need for healing rest on a regular basis. The challenge is to set aside time for healing rest. Most of us can't set aside an entire day per week. The next best thing is to create Sabbath moments daily, ways of taking time out to center and to go deeper into our faith, and to connect ever more strongly to God.

I like to find a place where I can sit by myself, often first thing in the morning and, if possible, again in the later afternoon or early evening, as many spiritual teachers suggest. Sitting up straight is important because it provides a physical sensation of steadiness and of centeredness. I light a candle as a way of making visible the center I am seeking. Then I close my eyes and notice my breath moving in and out of my body. Keeping my back straight, I select a word from my Christian tradition, such as Jesus, love, or spirit, to help me to stay in that center. When I experience the natural wanderings of my mind, I focus on my chosen word to help keep my mind in a place of rest and of healing. I also try to be aware of the thoughts and feelings I have, the way my body feels each time I use this word to return to the focus on centering. This word becomes a form of prayer, and it permits my mind to open to the mind and heart of God. In time, the practice of this centering prayer deepens and strengthens my relationship to God through the mind and heart of Jesus, who lives with me and guides me in the path of Oneness.

I often conclude my Sabbath moment with a spoken prayer, including, for example, the names of people in need, the state of the world, and the care of the earth. Then, as I slowly open my eyes, the first thing I see is the flame of the candle that helped invite me into the place of centering.

Journaling

Reading scripture and allowing it to "speak" is another practice I use to deepen a Sabbath moment. Traditionally, this is known in prayer as *lectio divina*, but I use it as a way to frame my journal entries. The basic principle behind *lectio divina* is that scripture almost always suggests ideas and questions that need our thought, and that when we ponder these texts, they contribute to our healing as we grow spiritually.

I start by picking a scripture passage, thinking about it, then finding a word or phrase that gets my attention. Then I write in my journal about my interest in it. Here's one example.

I chose the Parable of the Prodigal Son (Luke 15:11–32). On first read, it seems to be a story about a bad son, a good son, and a generous parent. The younger son demands his inheritance, takes it to a "distant country," spends it all, "comes to himself," and realizes that he has to go out and make a living. He gets a terrible job that doesn't even pay enough to survive and finally decides to go home and see if his father will hire him to work on the family farm. The father welcomes him back with a great celebration, but the older son is deeply resentful. He says that he has always been good, always obeyed the commands of the parent, and yet no party was ever thrown for him.

As I read the passage and thought about it and then read it again, I looked for a word or a phrase that attracted my attention. I settled on the father's words of greeting for his youngest son: "for this my son was dead and is alive again, was lost and now is found." As I wrote those words in my journal, I realized just how unusual this father's behavior was. Instead of being angry, he forgave his son and made real that moment of forgiveness by giving a lavish party. What would make him do that? I began to realize that he had reached a level of identity that did not have himself at the absolute center. He had risen above that to a place where forgiveness reflected a higher level of spiritual awareness. I began to see the parable as a story about levels of spiritual awareness ranging from the narrowest identity, framed only by self-interest, to the highest, where forgiveness is not only possible but can expand awareness and create a new identity. The process of journaling with scripture gave shape to my spiritual questions and increased my own level of spiritual awareness.

Outside the Box

While Sabbath moments and journaling are two practices that draw on the traditions of Christianity, I believe there are many occasions during an ordinary day that can be turned into spiritual practices. For me, these are the moments or occasions during the day when what I am doing helps me move forward, go deeper, or gives me hope. These moments can come from surprising places. For example, I actually enjoy washing the dishes, both because I am contributing to the "economy" of our household and because I can see results so clearly. Washing dishes gives me a sense of forward movement.

Moving forward, going deeper into the thoughts and feelings of the soul, and trying to see hope in the midst of despair are all forms of spiritual experience. When I asked myself recently, "Where do I experience this in my life?" I realized that singing and playing music are spiritual practices for me. Music gives me the greatest sense of connecting to God, of connecting my spirit to God's spirit. The more I thought about it, I realized that there are three specific types of music that do this for me:

> *"Getting out of Egypt" music:* What I call "getting out of Egypt" music is music with a strong backbeat that gives a feeling of moving forward unambiguously. I use the term *Egypt* as a metaphor for a place of imprisonment, just as it was, literally, for four hundred years for the Hebrew slaves before they escaped in the great story of the Exodus. I like that sense of moving forward in music because it feels to me, as a person of faith, that I am not merely moving forward but I am moving toward something very important and healing. The first time I heard

music that gave me this sense was in July of 1955, when Bill Haley and the Comets came out with "Rock Around the Clock." I was trying to find the *Lone Ranger* program on my radio, accidentally tuned in a St. Louis station, and the rest is history! Moving forward. Getting unstuck. Moving toward something good, something further ahead on your spiritual path. That's my kind of music.

"Stepping down in" music: For me, this kind of music feels like walking down stairs. It's similar to "getting out of Egypt" music, but in this case, instead of going forward, the music is going deeper, which gives a stronger sense of centering. Most of the time "stepping down in" music is more reflective and slower than "getting out of Egypt" music. If you have access to a piano, go to it and find the white note that is middle C. Play it and then, moving to the left, strike the next three white notes: B, A, G. The sequence sounds like walking down the stairs, going deeper. My all-time favorite song like this is an old blues song called "Nobody Knows You When You're Down and Out." Bessie Smith made it popular, and Eric Clapton has an excellent version. I also like John Denver's "This Old Guitar." Both songs take me down in.

The blues: Without the experience of despair, there would be no cause to write a blues song. But without hope, there would be no way to play or sing it. What particularly carries the sense of hope overcoming despair is the sound of notes being "bent." These bent or "blue" notes are produced in singing or playing by altering the pitch up or down. That movement gives me a feeling that space is being created and a window is being opened, a window that gives me a glimpse beyond and a feeling of hope.

I mention these examples not because I expect most people to play music, but because these experiences convey my belief that spiritual practices can happen "outside the box." I fully embrace the idea that many things in life can surprise us, strengthen us, and reassure us as we discover that they can actually be spiritual practices.

Rabbi Ted's Practices

I consider myself very lucky to be able to work in a way that allows me to focus on what is most important in my life. In many ways, my spiritual practice is my life, and my life, my spiritual practice. I get to meditate with people, to sing and talk about the reality of Oneness, of interconnectedness, and to celebrate the One Life we share. And there are private moments, as well as time with my family and friends, all of which have the possibility of becoming part of the spiritual grounding of my life.

A Prayer of Gratitude to Begin the Day

In Jewish tradition, the first words to be spoken each morning upon awakening are these words of gratitude:

> *Modeh* [women say *Modah*] *ani l'fanecha, Melech chai v'kayam, sheh-heh-che-zarta bi nishmati b'chemlah, rabbah emunatecha.*

> I give thanks in Your Presence, Universal Creative and Sustaining Presence, for You have mercifully returned my soul to me; great is Your faithfulness.

No matter what concerns awaken with the day, I strive to remind myself that the day itself is a gift, a great and wonderful gift. I have been given the day as an opportunity for awakening, for celebrating, for sharing, and for healing. The prayer reminds me that I want to remain more awake to what each moment asks of me. To what shall I be called this day?

A Focus for Meditation

The words with which I first practiced Jewish meditation in the early 1970s are still with me in meditation today. As I wrote earlier, (YISS-rah-EYL) the *Sh'ma* is the central affirmation of Jewish tradition and identity:

> *Sh'ma Yisrael, Adonai Eloheinu, Adonai Echad.*
> (Sh'MA YISS-rah-EYL, Ah-doh-NAI Eh-loh-HEY-nu,
> Ah-doh-NAI eh-CHAD.) The "ch" in *Echad* is a gutteral
> sound.

> Listen, Israel, the Eternal is our God, the Eternal is One.
> *Deuteronomy 6:4*

Here are some of the practices based on the *Sh'ma* that have been of special value to me since I began using the *Sh'ma* as a focus for meditation nearly forty years ago:

Simple recitation: The simplest meditation consists of simply repeating the words themselves. Without worrying about meaning, simply trust the sounds and the rhythms, and focus on them. While sitting and while walking, recite the *Sh'ma*. Allow the *Sh'ma* to support your unique spiritual journey.

Just listen ... and breathe: The first word of the *Sh'ma* means "Listen." One of the simplest and yet most profound meditative techniques involves focusing on this single word and repeating it gently and silently. Sometimes repeating it only on the out-breath can be helpful.

You can do this even now, as you are reading this. Take a gentle breath, and as you release it, repeat the sound *Sh'ma* silently. You may notice that there is a natural resting place after exhaling and a resting place after inhaling. Breathe in and rest ... breathe out *Sh'ma* and rest ... breathe in and rest ... breathe out *Sh'ma* and rest ...

> *The whole is greater than the sum of its parts:* There are two basic ways to silently repeat the *Sh'ma* as a focus for meditation. One way is to connect the words to the breath, and the other is to repeat the words independent of the breath. For many, utilizing the breath is very helpful at the beginning of this practice, and then later releasing the association to the breath allows yet another level of deepening.

If you choose to connect your meditation to the breath, it is easy to breathe in as you silently repeat the word *Sh'ma* ... breathe out *Yisrael* ... breathe in *Adonai* ... breathe out *Eloheinu* ... breathe in *Adonai* ... breathe out *Echad* ... and keep repeating the sequence as long as you desire.

> *Meditating on the heart of the Sh'ma:* The "heart" of the *Sh'ma* consists of the central two words, *Adonai Eloheinu*. In this meditative practice, begin with the entire six words of the *Sh'ma*—*Sh'ma Yisrael Adonai Eloheinu Adonai Echad*. Repeat the cycle gently, slowly, evenly, either attached to the breath or not. And then move more deeply into the heart of the *Sh'ma*, the central two words, *Adonai Eloheinu*. Repeat them easily. Slowly. Quietly. Syllable by syllable. Keep repeating these two words until you're ready to begin returning to normal wakeful awareness. Then gently return to the six words of the *Sh'ma*.

A Special Blessing

There is a blessing that I recite whenever I am aware of doing something for the first time. I also use it when I am aware that I have slipped from the awareness of connection and experience the harsher aspects of my separate self. This blessing is called the *Shehechiyanu*:

> *Baruch atah Adonai, Eloheinu Melech ha-olam, sheh-heh-chiyanu, v'kee'manu, v'hee-gee-yanu laz'man ha-zeh.*

> Blessed are You, Holy One, Eternal Creative Presence, the One awakening within each of us as our God, Who keeps us in Life always, Who supports our unique life path, and Who brings us to this very moment for blessing.

At moments of celebration, the words of this blessing enhance the awareness of that rejoicing. At times of difficulty, the words call me to remember that I am always connected to the Source of all Life.

Traditionally, Jews are called on to recite one hundred blessings each day. If we read through the prayer book for each of the daily services, we accomplish that task. For me, that kind of formal worship is not conducive to my remembering. Instead, I seek to find the blessing in each moment I meet. And when I cannot feel them, I listen for those who do, that I might silently say, "Amen." It is taught that if you hear a blessing and say, "Amen," it is as if you recited the whole blessing yourself.

Study

Learning is part of the Jewish Way, and it is so important that it is included in the great teaching by the first-century sage, Rabbi Hillel. When asked by a non-Jew to tell him the essence of Judaism while he stood on one foot, Hillel replied, "Do not do unto others that which is hateful to you. That is the whole of Torah. All the rest is commentary. Go now and learn."

Each week, there is a portion of the Torah read in the synagogue and studied there and at home, so that each year we read through the first five books of the Hebrew Bible. One of my disciplines is the study of Torah, and I remind myself that if I only find in the portion what I found before, I have not really grown. Torah is a spiritual literature, reflecting the spiritual nature of the ones through whom that text flowed. And the nature of Spirit is ever-expanding, ever-evolving. There is always more.

You can find a table of Torah portions by searching for weekly Torah readings on the Internet. Studying those chapters each week is part of my spiritual practice. The portions are actually broken down into daily readings, but most of the time I focus on the whole portion.

The Practice of Kindness

The practice of kindness is called *gemilut chasadim,* meaning "acts of loving-kindness," and it is the expression of compassion through thought, intention, word, and acts in the world. Jewish tradition teaches that the study of spiritual literature and the practice of prayer and meditation lead to acts of loving-kindness in the world.

Kindness becomes an intention. Although I do my best to remember this during my day, I most need it during the moments of forgetting. When another driver cuts me off on the freeway, or refuses to move into the intersection when wanting to turn left at a traffic signal, when things just don't go the way I anticipate or desire, when others become angry at me or I at them, I strive to remember: it's time for kindness.

Kindness of thought, of word, and of action reinforces spiritual growing. Harshness detracts from spiritual consciousness. So kindness becomes a spiritual practice on a daily basis. I strive to appreciate the Divine Presence awakening through each and every one of us, whether we are aware of it at the moment or not. Perhaps my appreciation can help in others' awakening.

Nighttime Forgiveness Practice

There is a remarkable prayer to be recited before bed that appears in many traditional Jewish prayer books. It is meant to help us release any resentments that we have built up during the day. Here are the words that I repeat. Sometimes my wife and I take turns reading it to each other before going to sleep at night.

> *Ribono shel olam ...*
>
> *Holy Presence of the Universe, I now forgive all who have hurt me, all who have done me wrong, whether deliberately or by accident, whether by word, by deed, or by thought, whether against my pride, my person, or my property, in this incarnation or in any other. May no one be punished on my account.*
>
> *And may it be Thy Will, Eternal One, my God and the God of my fathers and mothers, that I be no more bound by the wrongs that I have committed, that I be free from patterns that cause pain to me and to others, that I no longer do that which is evil in Thy sight.*
>
> *May my past failings be wiped away in Your great Mercy, Eternal One, and may they not increase pain and suffering.*
>
> *Let my words, my thoughts, my meditations, and my acts flow from the fullness of Your Being, Eternal One, Source of my being and my Redeemer.*

Prayer, meditation, study, and action in the world—these are the aspects of my spiritual path as it unfolds every day. Those who know me, who know how caught up I tend to get in the trivia and the busyness of my life, appreciate that this is my intention, even if it is not always my reality. But this is the nature of a spiritual path: It leads beyond itself, always expanding our awareness of the One we share.

Sheikh Jamal's Practices

Muslims believe that human beings are inherently good, but that we carry a "slinking whisperer" in our hearts (114:4). The temptations of the slinking whisperer can be hard to resist, and as a result of the tension between our higher and baser natures, the ego progresses, according to the Qur'an, through three stages of development. In the initial stage, the ego tends to be a commanding master, but as we learn to shine the light of awareness on it, it becomes less insistent and domineering. In the second stage, the ego is willing to accept responsibility and learns to make wiser choices. In the third stage, having learned the art of making beneficial choices, the ego is at peace and the self identifies with its true essence.

The work of self-awareness is a critical part of our spiritual practice. "Know yourself and you shall know your Sustainer," said the Prophet Muhammad. Without this work we are stuck in negative patterns, filled with excuses, unaware of attachments, and overwhelmed by anxieties and fears. When we shine the light of awareness on them, we can see them for what they are, and their mysterious power over us begins to diminish. We feel freer, better able to align our personalities with our higher selves.

If the light of awareness is infused with compassion and gentleness, it becomes graced with the mystery and beauty of sacredness. In my own life and in my practice with clients, I often use two exercises to strengthen the spiritual muscles of compassion for self: sacred naming and sacred journaling.

Sacred Naming

When I was young, my parents taught me to choose a term of endearment that would evoke feelings of mercy and compassion for myself when I was feeling down about things that had happened or things that I had said or done. I decided to call myself "Brother Jamal," and whenever I use that term, I feel a wave of mercy wash over me, making me better able and willing to deal with feelings of pain or conflict.

When I introduce this spiritual practice to others, I ask them to consider a word or sentence that resonates for them. The possibilities are endless: *beloved, child of grace, funny girl, dude*—anything that makes your heart smile and softens the sharpness of your critical self.

Since we humans are almost always talking to ourselves, I suggest using this technique of sacred naming whenever we become aware that our internal dialogue has taken a negative turn. Many times it is the voice of the ego judging, criticizing and blaming, often judging others, but just as often criticizing ourselves. When we interject our sacred name and continue the conversation, the content, tone, and direction of the dialogue change. When we invoke compassion, our higher self emerges and takes over the dialogue with our baser self. The ego melts in the face of compassion.

This process can also be carried out in the form of writing. I usually start by writing, "At this time I am feeling …" and continue with the flow until I have poured my feelings out on paper. I give myself permission to acknowledge and express my difficult feelings fully. I take a minute or two to read what I have written and just be present with the feelings I have expressed. Then I invoke my higher self by writing, "Dear one [or my chosen endearment], this is your higher self." Addressing the ego with tenderness, I say something like, "Thank you for allowing yourself to feel. I am sorry you are suffering. I have read carefully what you have written, and I want to tell you …" I am often amazed at the insights, nurturance, and healing that flow from my pen to my heart.

Sacred Journaling

I find that a major method of maintaining vigilance over the *nafs,* the little self, is to keep a notebook or journal. I try to be continuously aware of my speech and actions, and keep notes about the qualities I discover in myself—both qualities that reflect my higher self and those that reflect my *nafs*. I glorify God for my good qualities and look for ways to deepen them. As for shortcomings, I acknowledge them with compassion for myself and remember that these qualities do not reflect my true self.

Then, with awareness and discipline, I try to diminish them. One technique I use is what Sufis call "therapy of opposites." When I am inclined to be miserly and selfish, I make deliberate efforts to engage in acts of generosity. With mindfulness, I go out of my way to help a neighbor or give money to someone in need. If I experience resistance and awkwardness, I need to be gentle and merciful with myself. I find that through persistent practice of compassionate self-awareness, the negative attribute of my personality dissolves, and I evolve slowly but surely into my divine nature. If I slip up, I know that the Light of the Heavens and the Earth is boundlessly merciful. I am compassionate with myself and persist. I trust the Universe to provide me with a stream of opportunities to help me build my spiritual muscles and connect me to my divine attributes.

Opening the Heart

In Islamic spiritual terms, God resides in the throne of the heart; astonishingly and mysteriously, the Divine Heart is in the human heart. Our spiritual task is to open a passageway from heart to Heart: "Open up my heart to Thy Light" (20:25, trans. Asad). There are five techniques that can help. While they are simple, they are not necessarily easy. They require practice and persistence.

> *Be silent:* The Qur'an tells us that God is closer to us than our own jugular vein (50:16). When I am able to steady the dizziness of my wandering thoughts and not be distracted by what Rumi calls the "carnal screams of our life," only then I can hear God's tender whispers of guidance and

support. Only then can I feel the unspeakable joy of God's presence.

Listen to the heartbeat: This simple exercise requires nothing more than closing my eyes and focusing on my heart. I embrace the infinite and mysterious spaciousness of my heart. As I begin to listen to the magical beat and rhythm, I abide with it. If my attention wavers, I gently bring it back to my heartbeat. Over time, I not only feel an extraordinary centeredness and grounding, but I also experience closeness to Mystery.

Love the heart: This technique takes the practice of focusing on the heartbeat a step further. As I become increasingly mindful of my heart beating in my chest, I speak words of love and beauty to my heart. I keep telling my heart, "I love you" or "I cherish you." (If you try this practice and find that it feels awkward at first, know that with repetition it will come to feel more natural. If words of love don't resonate for you, try speaking words of simple gratitude. Tell your heart, "Thank you … I am so grateful … thank you.") The ultimate goal of this practice is to express love and devotion to the Divine Heart residing in the human heart. People who have practiced this technique for years report that in times of difficulty, astonishingly, a voice from within calls out, "I love you!" and they find themselves wrapped in an exquisite embrace of love and comfort.

Purifying the heart: For me the best way to purify the heart in Islam is to do the body prayer five times a day. This practice requires discipline and commitment. Facing in the direction of Mecca, I stand in the presence of Majesty, bow, prostrate, and kneel. I recite Qur'anic words of praise and gratitude to God. Spiritual teachers like to say that one prostration of prayer to God frees us from a thousand prostrations to our egos. A number of non-Muslims in our community incorporate a modified version of the body prayer in their spiritual practice. Once or twice a day, they bow and prostrate to Elohim, Jesus, or Spirit by touching the floor with their foreheads and by expressing words of praise and gratitude to Divinity. The practice, they say, gives them a feeling of unspeakable closeness to God.

Embracing joys and sorrows: The primary way, for me, to open the heart is to embrace not only the joys but also the sorrows of life. The Qur'an says that it is God who has created feelings and has given us the capacity to shed tears (23:78 and 53:43). Feelings are sacred, begging to be acknowledged and integrated. While it requires courage and patience to embrace difficult feelings, the rewards are phenomenal. Once the heart breaks open, I gratefully realize that, by grace of God, there is so much more space for love, compassion, forgiveness, intimacy, and passion to flow in.

Sacred Holding

The crucial practice of embracing difficult feelings, little by little, is a Sufi practice taught by my grandfather called "sacred holding." I have found that by doing this practice, my pain, sadness, and anger become integrated and transformed into a source of empowerment, wholeness, and blessing. Something deepens in me. I draw closer to Mystery.

I often teach this six-step process in my workshops. Though it requires a little time and a quiet space, it is an amazing way to open the passageway between human heart and Divine Heart.

The first step is to give yourself permission to feel your feelings, no matter how difficult or awkward. Gently and with a sense of balance, magnify them a bit. (Try not to overdo this.) Do this little by little, always with compassion for yourself. Remind yourself that all feelings are sacred.

Then ask yourself where you experience the feelings in your body. Feelings do have a resting place and are experienced as sensations in the body. Patiently direct your consciousness to locating them.

Once you have located the feelings, acknowledge the sensations and embrace them with your consciousness, again with mercy for yourself. Continuously shine the light of awareness on them and abide with them. If the sensations move to another location, move your attention to that new place.

Now ask yourself questions about the physical characteristics of the sensations that you are holding in your body. Do they have a color? Spend some time with this question and be mindful of what you perceive. Do the same with these other questions. Do they have a shape, texture, temperature, and weight? Be lovingly mindful of the physical characteristics of your feelings.

Next, tenderly direct some questions to that center of sensation in your body. Ask it, "Do you have a message for me? Are you trying to convey something important to me?" Make sure that you are truly listening. Then ask, "How may I love and integrate you?" Again, listen in respectful silence.

Finally, make an intention as you inhale and exhale to allow your breath to flow through that physical locus of your feelings. Allow the Divine Breath to caress that focal point, healing, integrating, and transforming the difficult feelings.

Healing through Spiritual Practices

In a conversation with David Crumm on ReadTheSpirit.com, Rev. Barbara Brown Taylor made a fascinating statement about her book *An Altar in the World: A Geography of Faith,* which explores many different spiritual practices: "I have found new friends in some Jewish communities, some Buddhist communities.... I have tried to write the kind of book that would appeal to all of these communities, because sometimes they are the same community.... I did this intentionally by writing a book about spiritual practice because I have high hopes that practice can bring us together where doctrine divides us."

In our interfaith work, we have found this to be wonderfully true. When we participate in each other's rituals and practices, we move beyond the understanding of the mind and begin to understand with the heart.

One way in particular that we have found for the three Abrahamic faiths to meet each other and either begin or deepen the interfaith dialogue is through the celebration of what we call a Three-Day Shabbat. Friday is the main gathering day for Muslims, Friday evening and Saturday is Shabbat for Jews, and Sunday, although technically the Day of Resurrection, is celebrated as the Sabbath in the Christian community.

A Three-Day Shabbat invites a sharing of our rituals toward common purpose. The nature of the program you might create will depend on the degree to which interfaith dialogue already is taking place, but the design is simple and natural. The community gathers at noon on Friday, either at a mosque or at another place where Muslim prayer will take place. Christians and Jews can either witness or share the prayer with Muslims, and at a simple lunch afterward, talk together about the nature of that experience. Friday night or Saturday morning would be the sharing of the Jewish Shabbat, and Sunday morning would be Christian worship. No one would be asked to "water down" their tradition, but each would celebrate the deepest yearnings of their own faith. Saturday and Sunday afternoons can provide further time for study and for discussion.

Sometimes, we imagine a community-wide Three-Day Shabbat that happens twice each year, with participants learning how to deepen the experience each time. This would be a true expression of stage 5 on the interfaith journey, exploring spiritual practices from other traditions. All would not only witness the ways in which the three Abrahamic traditions celebrate their special day of the week, but potentially everyone could enter into the experience themselves.

Whether individually or as a community, no matter what the foundation of our path, the spiritual practices of meditation, journaling, contemplating, and study can all support us in deep ways—no matter their faith of origin. There is but one caveat: we have to practice them. It's an old story. It's the answer to a visitor to New York City who asks, "How do you get to Carnegie Hall?"

"Practice, practice, practice!"

Well, that is pretty spot-on concerning the spiritual journey. So we encourage you to take some time with a practice that makes sense to you. Journal your experiences so that you can better witness your process and your progress. Be aware of resistances that may arise. Most important, be aware of changes you perceive within yourself or in the world around you.

Spiritual practices from a wealth of traditions can help awaken you to your deeper spiritual identity, to the fullness of your human potential. Because this is so, the very nature of your experience in the world can shift. Not only will you find a rejuvenation of soul, of mind, and of body, but this final stage of the interfaith process will allow you to celebrate this healing together with other people on the interfaith journey.

7

THERE IS ALWAYS MORE

The Conclusion Is Also a Beginning

My call for a spiritual revolution is not a call for a religious revolution. Nor is it a reference to a way of life that is somehow otherworldly, still less to something magical or mysterious. Rather it is a call for a radical reorientation away from our habitual preoccupation with self. It is a call to turn toward the wider community of beings with whom we are connected, and for conduct which recognizes others' interests alongside our own.

—Fourteenth Dalai Lama,
Ethics for the New Millennium

Authentic Spiritual Paths

Many people assume that the more they appreciate another's faith, the less attached they will be to their own, or that somehow their commitment to their own faith will diminish. Yet our experience demonstrates the exact opposite: Through our time together, we have each deepened our connection to our own tradition. The paradox is that the more we are willing to explore other traditions and recognize that they present authentic spiritual paths—avenues to a shared Universal—the more deeply we can understand our own paths. For example, Ted began wearing a *kippah*, the traditional head covering of the observing Jew, outside of worship and study— as well as while worshipping and studying—after he and Jamal started working together. Because Jamal, and many other Muslims, are easily identified by their dress, Ted chose to display more openly his own spiritual identity. Particularly in the months following 9/11, he wanted people to know that he, as a Jew, supported Jamal and the local Muslim community. Additionally, this physical reminder that we are always in the presence of God spoke to him of something his own tradition shared with Jamal's faith perspective, which resonated with the same belief.

Out of our work together, Don became interested in looking more closely into the writings of the Christian mystics, whose thinking parallels very closely the mystical traditions of Judaism and Islam, and this greater understanding of mysticism offered him deeper access to Christianity. For Jamal, the more he learned about Judaism and Christianity, the more deeply he understood insights in his own Holy Book, the Qur'an.

The famous professor of comparative religion Huston Smith wrote that when we view something only from one angle, we miss the deeper vision we can get only by viewing it from many perspectives. When people begin to share their faiths more deeply with others, it can be eye-opening to see that similar truths are expressed through different cultures, with different names, different stories, different characters, and different rituals. Often, people are amazed to find the same basic stories emerging from more than one tradition. Though our histories, our paths, our traditions may be different, when we recognize that we pursue the One Life we share, we find ourselves on common ground.

When the three of us hosted our year-long Interfaith Talk Radio show in Seattle, we had the remarkable opportunity of sharing, for an hour a week, teachings from many traditions. The guests we invited to join us on the show brought information from traditions other than our own. We talked about comfortable things and about things that were not so comfortable. We probably talked too much, but we also learned much. And we took special care to listen carefully to the experience of others and not be judgmental of other spiritual paths.

Our guests helped to reinforce one of our strongest convictions: There are many spiritual paths and *they are all authentic*. Many of them are extremely different from ours, different from what we are used to. On our show, we always looked for the universals that brought us together and the particular teachings in our traditions that supported those universals.

There are two images that we carry with us that describe the nature of our interfaith work to recognize the authenticity of our many spiritual paths. One is the metaphor of a mountain, and the other, the metaphor of an oasis. The images speak to us of the quest we have shared. Sometimes we climb to a shared height; other times, we dive down into the shared waters beneath us. Both images speak to our shared paths and hopes.

The Mountain of Wisdom

There was a town situated at the foot of a great mountain, and people thought of it as "their" mountain, a landmark of their town. It was so inspiringly beautiful to look at that most people never thought to climb it. There was a path, though, a single path, and some were curious enough to venture up. As they walked the path, they found the air a little fresher, the breeze a little cooler, and the view a little more panoramic. They were able to look down at their town, and from their new vantage point, they could see patterns of the streets and relationships of houses to each other that were not at all apparent at ground level. They climbed further and witnessed the rhythms of life in the town. People on the streets in the morning and in the afternoon almost seemed to flow like lifeblood through the arteries of the town.

And as some climbed still further and the circumference of the mountain began to decrease, they were surprised to see other people on other paths climbing up the very same mountain. The higher they went, the closer those other paths appeared, and it became possible for them to communicate with other climbers. It seemed that each path had begun in a different town, and the residents of each town thought theirs was the only town resting against the base of that mountain.

Some continued to climb until they got to a meadow where they could share together in person and contemplate the steep path to the summit. They quickly realized that they would fare far better if they helped each other to the top. In fact, they decided that the only way they could make it would be to cooperate and share the mountain-climbing skills that each group had gained. Before that final ascent, sitting together in the meadow, they told stories of their towns and of the paths each had taken. And they marveled at how strange and wondrous it was that all those paths led to a single summit.

The Secret of the Oasis

No sight is more welcome to a desert-dweller than the lush greenery of a desert oasis. Surrounded by miles and miles of dry sand, the oasis provides nourishment for body and soul. The people who dwelled at one such oasis may well have imagined that it was the only oasis in that part of the world. Surely, they might have thought, it was the most beautiful.

People at that oasis used to gather around the central pool. The water, stirred by faint breezes, calmed and comforted them. They shared stories of the development of their community surrounding that natural and ever-flowing spring. Most folks bathed in water drawn from that pool, and every once in a while, people would swim there.

Some men and women from that community got to wondering just how deep the water was, and they shared stories from their ancestors about the source of their oasis. From time to time, they dove down to seek the bottom, but none of them were able to hold their breath long enough to ever reach it.

Over time, the people developed techniques to increase the length of time they could remain under water. Occasionally, following a communal ritual, one or more practitioners of those breathing techniques would prepare themselves, receive the special blessings of the community, and then dive into the water. A few, able to hold their breath for a surprisingly long time, surfaced to tell of a great ocean that lay beneath their oasis.

Finally, there came a time when a diver did not resurface. The people waited by the shore until most gave up hope and drifted away to their tents with great sadness. But a few people remained by the pool, refusing to acknowledge that the diver was lost.

Many hours passed. The sun was already rising in the east when the diver leapt into the air. No—not only one—there were two divers celebrating their breath and splashing together.

"My brothers, my sisters," their own diver called out, "I found the entrance to another oasis! The ocean feeds many such pools of water. There are numerous such places as this! And I brought a friend from the other oasis I just found!"

Those on the shore were amazed and delighted, but it turned out that there were those in the town who immediately labeled the reports they received as hoaxes. "No," they said, "there is only one oasis, and ours is the only one that receives water from the deep ocean beneath us."

Inclusive Spirituality

For us, these beautiful stories point to the principle of inclusive spirituality. Many people use the word *spiritual* to refer to a special and deep experience or relationship. While we wouldn't wish to deny folks the use of that word, we mean something a little more specific. We like the term *inclusive spirituality* because it indicates the inclusivity we think the word *spirituality* refers to. Rabbi Ted likes to say that he has an imaginary scale in his head that allows him to assess the degree of spiritual awareness—inclusive spiritual awareness—that he is identified with at any given moment. The more he experiences separateness and fragmentation, lack of clarity and confusion, the less spiritual his awareness. The more he knows clarity, a strong sense of belonging, an awareness of oneness with others, with the world, or even with the universe, the more spiritual his consciousness.

For us, inclusive spirituality relates to the realization of Oneness, the Oneness toward which each of our faith traditions leads us. The One we seek is a shared One—there is only One. We believe the One, usually called "God" or "Allah" in our three faith traditions, is the One Universal Life that contains all that exists, yet is infinitely more than all that exists. To the extent that we realize ourselves as integral parts of that One, we are moving toward the spiritual side of the scale, as Rabbi Ted would describe it.

This inclusive spirituality is crucial because it leads to a very particular way of being in the world. When we are connected to each other and interconnected with all beings, we naturally begin to care better for others and for our planet. This spiritual consciousness allows us to see ourselves in all others and to understand that when we bring pain to another, we are actually bringing pain to ourselves. When we support another, we are also supporting ourselves. A strong ethic naturally flows from an inclusive spirituality, and this is the ethic we seek to celebrate together. In our interfaith work, we have realized again and again that the more deeply we share, the better we are able to appreciate the Universal we all seek to serve.

Don's Reflections

Much of my life has been a struggle between two strong opposing forces: the substance of the Gospel and the ways the religion of

Christianity has been constrained by political forces to support a status quo that too often guarantees poverty and many losses of civil rights, and supports the use of violence to solve problems.

Over the years we have been working together, my interfaith work with Ted and Jamal has helped me separate those two forces: to access a genuine pride in the substance of Jesus's teachings and to discover what in my life opposes the narrower interpretations of those teachings. In other words, my interfaith work has helped me to go deeper into my own faith as I have learned to appreciate the faiths of Ted and Jamal.

About five years ago, my church was invited to host a community interfaith Thanksgiving service. We had a curtain made to draw over the cross for interfaith situations where the cross would be either a distraction or simply inappropriate. When I suggested to the organizers of the event the possibility of covering the cross, they told me that their policy had always been to honor the tradition of the host congregation. So we did not cover the cross.

Instead, I made a statement at the beginning of worship that acknowledged my deep feelings for what the cross symbolized for me as a Christian. I also said that I understood that the cross had been a symbol of repression, hatred, and violence for many non-Christians. In a moment when we were gathered together to give thanks, I said that I looked forward to the day when the cross of Jesus would evoke feelings of oneness for all people. I looked forward to the day when the cross would point to the best of Jesus's teachings. I looked forward to the day when the violence and hatred associated with the cross would live only in history. It seemed to me to be a simple confession, and I was amazed afterward to hear of the deep appreciation of Christians and non-Christians who had come into our sanctuary to give thanks on that day.

I was actually surprised by what I said that night. It wasn't that it was untrue, or that I didn't feel it deeply. But by being able to welcome people of other faith traditions to a place I loved and to confess openly my longings for healing between and among the faiths, I reached a new place in my struggle between those two opposing forces: loving my tradition and feeling shame for the behavior that has often characterized the church in relation to other faiths. The moment helped me to build a bridge between that love and that shame. It was a healing moment for me.

Ted's Reflections

Thinking back over the years we three have worked together, I realize how much more aware I have become of the teachings on compassion that infuse the texts and traditions of Islam, and how teachings on love spring from the teachings of both the Jewish and the Christian Jesus. Just as in Judaism, there is often a disconnect between spiritual teachings and actions in the world in every tradition. Just as we must learn to differentiate between the essence of individuals and their acts, it is crucial to honor this difference between the specific actions of an adherent of a particular faith and the core teachings of that faith.

Working in an interfaith environment with Don and Jamal has deeply enriched my appreciation of my own tradition. Discovering the treasures of Christianity and Islam has led me to ask, "What does Judaism say about that?" And each time, I discover layers of spiritual wisdom that have deepened my respect for my own tradition and more deeply anchored my faith identity. As I look back over my career, over forty years now as a rabbi, I realize that I have often been called to serve in interfaith and multifaith environments, and it is in this context that my professional life has flowered most fully. There have always been significant numbers of non-Jews even within the congregations that I have served.

This year I am completing my tenure as the rabbi of the Bet Alef Meditative Synagogue, the congregation my wife and I created when we moved to Seattle sixteen years ago. Although I am excited about stepping more fully into an interfaith working environment, there are deep feelings of grief and loss that now rise within me. I am moving on from being the rabbi of meditative synagogues in Los Angeles and Seattle for well over thirty years—by far the greater part of my career so far as a rabbi.

Pastor Don and Sheikh Jamal continue to create a supportive place for me to share my feelings, and the wisdom that they bring is deeply healing. The fact that they have allowed me to support them in their journeys as well makes it easier for me to accept their counsel at times when I sorely need it.

Jamal's Reflections

Around the time that Don, Ted, and I were beginning to meet regularly, I attended a remarkable weeklong conference sponsored by *Yes!* magazine. There I heard a moving story about an African-American activist who, in his early youth, struck a white child for calling him "nigger." His father congratulated him when he heard about the deed, but his mother chided him tenderly. "What good did that do?" she asked. And then she continued, "Son, there has to be a better way." Her words resonated in the child's soul, and today he has dedicated his life to finding a better way. The words had a powerful impact on me, and they have become the driving force for my abiding and deepening interfaith relationship with Ted and Don.

Over the years, as our friendship has matured and we have become truly able to listen to each other and ask ourselves what it feels like to be the other, I have been inspired to reach out and apply a "better way" model to more difficult situations. And in my ministry I have made conscious efforts to use the precious insights and lessons I have learned in my relationships with my "Interfaith Amigos" to connect with those whose faith and opinions are markedly different from my own. I am thinking specifically of two evangelical Christians whom I can truthfully describe as being allergic to anything that has to do with Islam.

Over the years I have made conscious and persistent efforts to get to know these two people simply as friends, without any particular agenda, and two remarkable changes have occurred. The first is that my two friends are no longer anti-Islamic, and although we continue to disagree on scriptural matters, our disagreements no longer threaten our friendship. The second, and more remarkable, change is the way in which I myself have been transformed. I now realize that I had my own prejudices and stereotypes about right-wing Christians, and through my relationship with these two friends, I have come to see that they, too, have a deep sense of community and dedication to social justice and earth care. There are concrete and deeply meaningful projects we can collaborate on together.

I attribute this expanded consciousness in myself and in my ministry directly to the years of deepening relationships with my Interfaith Amigos. Rabbi Ted and Pastor Don are helping me to become more complete as a human being. Allah be praised for interfaith friendship and collaboration!

Honoring the Spirit

During the course of our interfaith journey, we have shared our stories and our deepest beliefs. We have wrestled with the problems and the promises of our faith traditions. We've gone beyond what is "safe" and moved to a different level of understanding in matters of the Middle East, where tensions and tempers are so very volatile. We have shared in each other's rituals and practices. In each of the five stages of the journey, we have been taking steps toward participating in an authentic spiritual experience through a tradition other than our own. This dimension of honoring the Shared Universal is the most challenging. Sometimes we are not able to appreciate the true depth of an experience until we actually *live* it. This was surely the case for us in what turned out to be a moment that integrated the major elements of our work together.

It started casually enough. Pastor Don had invited Ted and Jamal to help him lead a preworship forum on interfaith and social action at his church. About a month before that, Don realized that since the three of us were going to be at the church anyway, we could preach together on the golden rule as the sermon during worship. It seemed a safe enough topic.

But about two weeks before that service, Don realized that it was to be a communion Sunday. What to do about that? Then he remembered an experience from our Israel-Palestine trip where we had visited and taught at the Mount of the Beatitudes in Galilee in northern Israel. It had been a Friday afternoon, so Ted had concluded the teachings with the *Kabbalat Shabbat*, the traditional Welcoming of the Sabbath with wine and bread. Immediately, it had become clear to both Ted and Don how similar the ritual was to the traditional words and symbols of the sacrament of communion for Christians.

It had been a remarkable experience of the convergence of three traditions in that special moment and place. Jamal had also offered some reflections from his tradition, explaining the significance of Friday in Islam as the day God created Adam and his spouse, placed them in Paradise, and sent them to earth. Friday is also the Day of Judgment. On Fridays, when Muslims gather in community to praise and remember God, their prayers, especially at midday, have enhanced spiritual merit.

As Don sat reflecting on these events, he began to conceive of the possibility of including Rabbi Ted and Sheikh Jamal in the communion service. When he consulted with his colleagues on the pastoral staff at his church, they agreed that Ted and Jamal should be invited to serve the bread at the communion service. Step by step, little by little, that ritual moment was coming together.

But on the morning of that Sunday, as he was driving to church, Don began considering how he was going to introduce the communion moment. He certainly didn't wish to compromise the integrity of communion. The congregation would already have had a few surprises—leaders from the three Abrahamic faiths standing together, sharing the sermon, showing how the core teaching of the golden rule appeared in each tradition.

Don decided to start by introducing the "Open Table" to which his church welcomes all who wish to share. He reminded the congregation that communion is a sacrament, a moment when we are more deeply aware of the presence and the love of God through the person and teachings of Jesus. He talked about the way communion invites us all to experience forgiveness and, with love, to build loving community within a life of faith. The meal remembered and represented by the sacrament brings people together around a table, a ritual that exists in different ways in all religious traditions.

Then he said that Rabbi Ted and Sheikh Jamal would help serve the bread, and he asked people to reflect on how the presence of a rabbi and a sheikh could remind them of the greater embrace of a loving God and a welcoming community.

Pastor Don administered the sacrament at the communion table with the words from the United Church of Christ *Book of Worship*, "Through the broken bread we participate in the body of Christ," which is considered to be loving community, and "through the cup of blessing we participate in the new life Christ gives," indicating the openhearted love and compassion, which is identified as this new life.

Four pairs of people then took their places at the front of the sanctuary, one holding the cup and the other holding a basket of bread. Jamal and Ted stood with the center two pairs, each holding a basket of bread. Don had worried that too few people would accept the bread from Ted and Jamal, but actually very few came to his own basket of bread. The lines in front of Jamal and Ted were far longer than the others! Afterward, many expressed deep emotion about the reconciling presence of these two religious leaders in the midst of the sacrament.

For Don, it was a dramatic step away from a long history of repudiation of other faiths and a step toward honoring other spiritual paths without any need to feel coerced or defined by them. He knew that what happened that Sunday morning bridged the tension between the sacrament of communion as a symbol dedicated only to Christian community, and the need—suggested at the heart of Jesus's teachings—to be welcoming to all people. In the great mystery of the sacrament, this communion represented what Jesus taught: love, forgiveness, and loving community.

Jamal expressed his heartfelt gratitude to the congregation. He was aware of the deep spiritual significance of the sacrament to Christians, and as a Muslim, he felt blessed to participate because he felt a closeness to Jesus as a revered prophet, a connection with the ceremony, and a humble aspiration to experience community. A verse in the Qur'an tells us that if we remember God, God remembers us (2:152). The Prophet added that when people remember the Divine in community, God remembers them better. The sacred community created by this communion was truly a circle of love and beauty. Jamal was deeply moved by the large number of Christians enthusiastic about receiving communion from a Muslim, and it reaffirmed for him the power and majesty of hospitality and open-heartedness.

Perhaps the moment was most complicated for Rabbi Ted. Communion ceremonies clearly excluded him; taking communion meant that you were Christian. But over the years, Ted's relationship to Christians and to Christianity had changed. As he stood in Pastor Don's church that morning, he thought about the literal symbol: Jesus, a Jew, was sharing bread with other Jews. And he let that symbol expand so that a Jew was sharing bread with more than Jews, with those who would later be identified as his followers and be called Christians. While it was true that over centuries, the symbols of communion had developed deeper theological meanings and served to distinguish Christians, in the context of Pastor Don's teachings that morning, the bread and the wine could also be bread and wine. Like the bread and wine shared to welcome Shabbat, this bread and wine could celebrate sacred community and universal spiritual truth. This communion could represent a community, a place of nourishment, a place of forgiveness, of compassion, and of love. Standing at the front of that United Church of Christ, wearing *kippah* and *tallit*, Rabbi Ted was not Christian and was not pretending to be. He was a Jew honoring the church community with whom he was sharing. He was a Jew honoring the God of Love.

We are not recommending that interfaith participation in communion be standard practice. But the freedom to step into that place of Spirit on that communion Sunday was a blessing for the rabbi, for the sheikh, and, of course, for the pastor.

The Future of Interfaith Dialogue and Celebration

Interfaith dialogue and relationships have many stages, from separation and suspicion to embracing each other's spiritual practices. We have walked this path—from resistance to healing—and we have come, many times, to the sacred place of being humbly able to honor each other's spiritual paths. We have shared the stages of our particular journeys, but now it's in your hands. It's in your heart. You have precious opportunities of finding your own way on this interfaith journey. We hope what we have offered will support you on your unique path toward the deeper realization of the Life we all share.

We want to leave you with a few thoughts as you take those amazing steps on your own path.

> *Listen:* Practice listening to others and encourage them to share their stories. Begin dialogue on issues that are of greatest concern to you and to others. See how well you can identify with another's journey—particularly with those who seem most different from yourself. Allow yourself to move beyond suspicion and separation.

Learn: See if you can identify the shared universals that transcend every particular path but nourish us all. Look for the nature of oneness, love, compassion, and forgiveness in another's tradition. Learn how the particulars of a faith can, in fact, support universals we are all able to celebrate. As you inquire more deeply, you may learn more about your own tradition as well.

Discover: As you share, you will discover further opportunities for cooperation and collaboration. Learn to focus on these, and invite others to see them. Discover the ways in which you and those with whom you share can contribute to expanding levels of understanding and appreciation within your communities. This deeper level of discovery includes sharing both the comfortable and the uncomfortable aspects of our traditions.

Appreciate: The more you can be open to appreciating the particulars of another tradition, the better able you will be to perceive and to share the universals. The ground of mutual understanding can make it clear that no one needs to convert anyone else and that there are many authentic spiritual paths. Here you may find yourself moving beyond safe territory, but the groundwork you have created will support this deeper dimension of your journey.

Celebrate: Seek to celebrate the Universal together. If God is One, then we are all part of that One. Interfaith spirituality can allow you to support others as you climb to the top of the mountain. Taste the fruits that spring forth from your particular oasis. Celebrate an inclusive spirituality that can dispel distrust and suspicion and create pockets of peace wherever you go. Sometimes spiritual practices from another tradition can profoundly deepen your appreciation of your own faith.

It's time. We need each other more than ever, for we understand now how much we share. We have responsibilities to others and to our planet. Inclusive spirituality invites us to live less wastefully, to internalize simple truths of planetary ecology. It invites us to compassionate action in the world. It opens our hearts and promotes true compassion for others. It gives rise to visions of fulfilling basic human needs without resorting to violence. Inclusive spirituality naturally supports full access to all human and civil rights for everyone.

We are beings of deep faith. Our traditions provide us with communities and with continuity. But our traditions need to reach out beyond themselves. We are in this together.

It is our hope that our relationship and our teachings can be a gift to help you on this journey. As we strive to appreciate both the blessings and the griefs of each of our faiths, we dedicate ourselves to envisioning together a world of greater understanding, acceptance, compassion, and love. We dream of a world awakening to the essential Oneness that contains us all.

It's a matter of our survival.

Discussion Questions

1 **The Interfaith Journey**: *Stages of Interfaith Dialogue and*
   Collaboration

   - What does the word *interfaith* mean to you?

   - The stages of interfaith dialogue often begin with distrust
     and suspicion. Are there any religious groups with whom
     you experience this kind of distrust? What do you think
     might bridge the distance you feel?

   - Sometimes we tolerate each other, but do not know very much
     about the beliefs and rituals of someone of another religion.
     Have you ever been to a religious service of another faith? If
     so, what did that feel like? Have you ever welcomed another to
     an observance of your faith? What was that experience like?

   - What other faiths would you like to learn more about?

   - What differences or concerns get in the way for you when
     you think about interfaith relations? How might both your
     interests and concerns serve as a catalyst for your next step
     in exploring interfaith dialogue?

   - If you found something in another faith that resonated for
     you, would you be comfortable incorporating an aspect of
     that practice into your life and making it your own? What
     might that look like?

   - Do you think that interfaith exploration can lead to a water-
     ing down of an individual's faith identity? If so, how? Do you
     think such an exploration can deepen your faith identity?

- What opportunities are there in your community for meeting people of other faiths? How might you take advantage of these and explore them further?

2 **The Power of Our Stories:** *Moving Beyond Separation and Suspicion*

- In Pastor Don's journey to interfaith, he describes his experience of being born into privilege. How do you relate to the issue of privilege in your own life? Do you feel as if you are an "insider," or do you experience yourself on the "outside," looking in?

- Have there been special moments in your own life when you became aware of the suffering of others? What have been the consequences of those moments?

- Rabbi Ted shared his experience when he realized that he was a minority and related some of the painful experiences associated with that realization. Have you ever felt like a minority, an outsider, different? How has that experience influenced you?

- What is your relationship to some of the minorities in your community? How do you feel when you think about approaching them? What might your goals be in establishing such conversations?

- Sheikh Jamal shared his very special relationship with his parents. They were major teachers for him on his spiritual path. How have your parents influenced your own spiritual path? Are you following in their footsteps, or have you set out on your own? How has this affected your relationship with your parents?

- Sheikh Jamal said that, until 9/11, he never experienced discrimination as a Muslim, but he did experience discrimination as a person of color. How have you been aware of discrimination in your own life? Have you been able to allow your experience to sensitize you to the experience of others?

• The three authors mentioned the synchronicities that brought them together. How has synchronicity played a part in the significant relationships in your life? Are you aware of the special but surprising moments of meeting you have experienced?

• How have you become interested in issues of interfaith relations? Is this an important subject for you? What circumstances in your life have awakened your interest in other religions?

3 *The Core of Our Traditions:* Inquiring More Deeply

• Pastor Don believes in the transformative nature of love. In what ways have you experienced this? How do you see this power of love as a universal value?

• If Pastor Don sees love as the central focus of his Christian faith, does that mean Christianity "owns" love? What if several traditions share a common focus?

• Rabbi Ted talks about finding deeper meaning in words he had learned as a child. Are there texts, songs, or stories in which you are now able to find deeper meaning than they had for you when you first learned them? If so, how did that additional meaning become clear to you?

• Rabbi Ted shared an event that helped open him to a fuller vision of his spiritual identity and, through that, to deeper interfaith connections. Are there events in your own life that have enabled you to understand what you share with those of other faiths and traditions?

• Sheikh Jamal found himself experiencing the intensity of God's compassion even when going through an extremely difficult time of loss. When have you most been aware of universal compassion and love? When have you felt most distant from that love?

- Sheikh Jamal focuses on the virtue of compassion. Do you think that every spiritual path needs to reflect this virtue? Why?

- If you were to focus on one central teaching that has impacted you in your life, what would it be? How did you find that teaching? What has it meant for you?

4 **The Promises and Problems of Our Traditions:** *Sharing Both the Easy and the Difficult Parts*

- The authors talk about what they really like about their respective traditions. If you are a member of a faith tradition, can you share what especially appeals to you about your tradition? If you do not identify with a formal religion, what do you especially like about the way you have chosen?

- When you find things about your own path that you really like, do you feel that those things make your path better than any other? How do you handle questions from others about this?

- When you find awkward aspects of your path, do you find yourself avoiding them? Explaining them away? Can you share one aspect of your path that you find awkward? How might you interpret this in a more universal way?

- In what ways do you feel that your own path is misunderstood? What would you like others to know about your beliefs? Is there anything others do or say that particularly pains you?

- Are there issues you have with aspects of another faith? Would you be willing to share these concerns? If another has such concerns about your faith, what could you do to respond without defensiveness?

5 *Perspectives on Israel and Palestine: Moving Beyond Safe Territory*

- The pastor, the rabbi, and the sheikh traveled together to the land holy to each of them, but each perceived it very differently. The situation stimulated deeper conversation about some of the differences between them. Have you ever been on such a journey? When differences were discussed? Did they help people get closer, or did they provoke anger and greater distance?

- Pastor Don recognized the pain that has come to others from his Christian tradition. Perhaps all traditions can identify with this in their past. What are the difficulties that you perceive emerging from your religious tradition in the past or in the present? What pain has it caused others? Do you think such past pain can be healed?

- Rabbi Ted was struck by the paradoxical impact of religious institutions. He noted that although they develop to support a more universal spiritual experience, they tend to become focused on matters of their own survival. Does this reflect your experience with institutions of your faith? Are you aware of the purpose for which those institutions began?

- Sheikh Jamal was the only Muslim on this trip to the Holy Land, and he was immediately singled out for special questioning upon landing. To his surprise, the people from whom he had anticipated difficulty turned out to be supportive of his interfaith mission. How would you have felt watching him being pulled aside by security officers? Have you ever experienced unexpected hospitality?

- Sheikh Jamal was pained by the violence on both sides of the conflict between Israelis and Palestinians, and by the wall of separation that has been erected between the two peoples. He wondered about the walls that we create in our own lives, and the acts of violence we commit in our own "holy land." Are you aware of walls you build in your own world? What about cruel words and actions? How do you understand the walls of separation that people build to protect themselves from others?

- Each writer experienced Israel and Palestine differently. Which experiences did you most identify with? With which did you have greatest difficulty? Would you be interested in sharing such an interfaith journey—whether literally or metaphorically? With whom? What do you think it would take for you to prepare to move beyond "safe" territory to embark on such a journey?

6 *New Dimensions of Spiritual Identity*: Exploring Spiritual Practices from Other Traditions

- As you read about the spiritual practices in this chapter, which appeal to you the most? How can you imagine using them to deepen your interfaith understanding?

- What spiritual practices do you have that the authors have not discussed? How have they affected your life?

- Can you think of any things that you normally do in your life that are actually spiritual practices for you? How do you experience them as spiritual practices?

- The authors present spiritual practices from each of their traditions and believe such practices create the inclusiveness that supports positive change in the world. How do your spiritual practices translate into compassionate action in the world?

- You have seen how each of the Abrahamic traditions provides specific practices for helping us deepen our spiritual journey. Can you imagine practices that are not tied to a particular religion, but could be shared by all? What would it be like to see all of life as part of our spiritual practice?

7 *There Is Always More:* The Conclusion Is Also a Beginning

- The authors talk about the mountain of spiritual paths and spiritual purpose. Can you identify with this image? Where are you on that mountain? Where would you wish to be?

- In the oasis story, people tended to believe theirs was the only one connecting to the deepest source, just as in the early stages of the interfaith dialogue, some imagine that their faith alone is true. How would you encourage people to appreciate that there are many traditions connected to a single Source of life?

- The authors present *inclusive spirituality* as a spirituality shared by many different faiths and traditions. If this is so, what do you think is the value of having different religious traditions?

- One of the controversial moments the authors describe involves the sharing of communion. What were your impressions of this moment? What are your feelings about this kind of interfaith sharing?

- The end is always also the beginning. As you think about what you have felt and learned during your reading of this book, how have you changed? What new thoughts and ideas are emerging for you? Where will you go from here? As you contemplate that question, what possibilities come to mind? Can you imagine ways in which you can expand interfaith dialogue and understanding in your world? What are your hopes for what this could bring about?

Suggestions for Further Reading

Further Readings in Christianity

Bainton, Roland H., and Jaroslav Pelikan. *Christianity*. New York: American Heritage, 2000.

Borg, Marcus J. *The Heart of Christianity: Rediscovering a Life of Faith*. San Francisco: HarperSanFrancisco, 2003.

Brown Taylor, Barbara. *An Altar in the World: A Geography of Faith*. New York: HarperCollins, 2009.

Butler Bass, Diana. *Christianity for the Rest of Us*: *How the Neighborhood Church Is Transforming the Faith*. New York: HarperCollins, 2006.

Crossan, John Dominic. *The Birth of Christianity: Discovering What Happened in the Years Immediately After the Execution of Jesus*. New York: HarperCollins, 1998.

Guthrie, Shirley C. *Always Being Reformed: Faith for a Fragmented World*, 2nd ed. Louisville: Westminster John Knox Press, 2008.

Tickle, Phyllis. *The Great Emergence: How Christianity is Changing and Why*. Grand Rapids, Mich.: Baker Books, 2008.

Volf, Miroslav. *Exclusion and Embrace: A Theological Exploration of Identity, Otherness, and Reconciliation*. Nashville: Abington Press, 1996.

Further Readings in Islam

Ali-Karamali, Sumbul. *The Muslim Next Door: The Qur'an, the Media and That Veil Thing*. Ashland, Ore.: White Cloud Press, 2008.

Armstrong, Karen. *Muhammad: A Prophet for Our Time*. New York: HarperCollins Publishers, 2006.

Dardess, George. *Meeting Islam: A Guide for Christians*. Orleans, Mass.: Paraclete Press, 2005.

Firestone, Reuven. *An Introduction to Islam for Jews*. Philadelphia: Jewish Publication Society of America, 2008.

Rahman, Jamal. *The Fragrance of Faith: The Enlightened Heart of Islam*. Watsonville, Calif.: The Book Foundation, 2004.

Rahman, Jamal, Kathleen Schmit Elias, and Ann Holmes Redding. *Out of Darkness Into Light: Spiritual Guidance in the Quran with Reflections from Jewish and Christian Scriptures*. New York: Morehouse Publishing, 2009.

Further Readings in Judaism

Dosick, Wayne D. *Living Judaism: The Complete Guide to Jewish Belief, Tradition, and Practice*. New York: HarperCollins, 1998.

Falcon, Ted. *Journey of Awakening: Kabbalistic Meditations on the Tree of Life*. Seattle: Skynear Press, 2001.

Falcon, Ted, and David Blatner. *Judaism For Dummies*. Hoboken, N.J.: John Wiley & Sons, 2001.

Kaplan, Aryeh. *Meditation and Kabbalah*. New York: Samuel Weiser, 1985.

Kushner, Lawrence. *Jewish Spirituality: A Brief Introduction for Christians*. Woodstock, Vt.: Jewish Lights, 2001.

Matlins, Stuart M., ed. *The Jewish Lights Spirituality Handbook: A Guide to Understanding, Exploring & Living a Spiritual Life*. Woodstock, Vt.: Jewish Lights, 2001.

Robinson, George. *Essential Judaism: A Complete Guide to Beliefs, Customs & Rituals*. New York: Pocket Books, 2001.

Schoen, Robert. *What I Wish My Christian Friends Knew about Judaism*. Chicago: Loyola Press, 2004.

Further Readings in Interfaith Dialogue and Spirituality

Chittester, Joan. *Welcome to the Wisdom of the World*. Grand Rapids, Mich.: Eerdmans, 2007.

Heckman, Bud, with Rori Picker Neiss. *InterActive Faith: The Essential Interreligious Community-Building Handbook*. Woodstock, Vt.: SkyLight Paths, 2008.

Idilby, Ranya, Suzanne Oliver, and Priscilla Warner. *The Faith Club: A Muslim, A Christian, A Jew—Three Women Search for Understanding*. New York: Free Press, 2006.

Karabell, Zachary. *Peace Be upon You: The Story of Muslim, Christian and Jewish Co-Existence*. New York: Random House, 2007.

Littell, Franklin H. *The Crucifixion of the Jews: The Failure of Christians to Understand the Jewish Experience*. Macon, Ga.: Mercer University Press, 2000.

Matlins, Stuart M., and Arthur J. Magida, eds. *How to Be a Perfect Stranger: The Essential Religious Etiquette Handbook*. 4th ed. Woodstock, Vt.: SkyLight Paths, 2006.

Mays, Rebecca Kratz, ed. *Interfaith Dialogue at the Grassroots*. Philadelphia: Ecumenical Press, Temple University, 2008.

Smock, David R. *Interfaith Dialogue and Peacebuilding*. Washington, D.C.: United States Institute of Peace, 2002.

Acknowledgments

We don't know whether the most important acknowledgment goes first or last, so we are simply mentioning a few very special people who supported us in writing this book.

Amy Frykholm spent a weekend with us over Passover and Easter in the spring of 2008, and her article about us was the cover story of the August 26, 2008 issue of *Christian Century*. We have learned from Amy's lively and clear writing, and we are grateful most of all for her friendship.

When Marcia Broucek, acquisitions editor for SkyLight Paths, read that article, she contacted us about our reference to writing a book. She became our editor, and though we imagine that she does exactly what an editor is supposed to do, for us it often seemed like magic. She restored order when we had lost it (without even knowing it) and had an uncanny ability to help each of us develop our separate voices. We are responsible for anything lacking in these pages. Marcia shares with us the responsibility for all that speaks more clearly, and we are grateful.

At the time the article was published in *Christian Century*, we were rehearsing for an evening of spiritual theater that was set in motion to celebrate Ted's fortieth anniversary as a rabbi. Arne and Claire Zaslove, very well-known theater people in Seattle, directed and developed the script. Arne helped us work together in a totally new way (such as singing "Stop in the Name of Love!" complete with choreography), and Claire provided outstanding lyrics and words for us to perform.

We intend to continue our relationship with all these special people and wish to clearly express our gratitude for all they have done to support us. We are hopeful that in some measure we are supporting them as well.

We each thank our two partners in this adventure for their companionship and steadfastness. We have become each other's clergy, and we continue to learn from each other. Our voices are distinct, our traditions very different, yet we are part of one evolving and expanding celebration of the One. We delight in sharing this celebration as fully as we are able.

Don

Judy Mackenzie has been a support and cherished companion for forty-three years! God bless you, dear! David McCracken and Bud Thompson provided very helpful feedback for my parts of the book. My colleagues on the staff and the congregation at University Congregational United Church of Christ in Seattle gave me a foundation and a home for my involvement in the work of interfaith. And David and Fran Korten at the Positive Futures Network have created a vision of a better world to which interfaith can contribute.

Ted

I have been privileged to begin two meditative synagogues, Makom Ohr Shalom in Los Angeles (1978) and Bet Alef in Seattle (1993). Cantor, now Rabbi Monty Turner in Los Angeles and Music Director Stephen Merritt in Seattle translated the teaching into song, and the communities grew vibrant. Members of both congregations helped draw forth the teachings that are reflected in this book. In the precious context of spiritual counseling and therapy, many clients over the years have given me the gift of their trust, and we have learned much together. And there are special people who have been my friends and teachers over these years, who have witnessed my stumbles and successes with open hearts. I am deeply grateful for all of you who have shared this remarkable journey with me.

My greatest joy in this work comes in witnessing awakening. Sharing a more inclusive awareness with others makes it all worthwhile. The greatest pain comes at moments of contracted awareness, when I know I am not awake, or, worse, when I think I am but I am not. During the past twenty-four years, Ruth Neuwald Falcon has been my wife and partner and has shared in the joys and the pains. Her presence makes it all bearable.

Jamal

I wish to express unbounded gratitude to the following: my beloved late parents, Ataur and Suraiya Rahman; my precious family, brother Kamal and his wife Naz, sister Aysu, daughter Kristina, nephews, nieces, and cousins; my cherished friends and colleagues, Karen Lindquist, Katayoon Naficy, Linda Jo Pym, Sally Jo Vargas, Faren Bachelis, Debra Lajmodiere, and Kate Elias, whose help in editing my pieces was invaluable; dear friends with whom I have shared classes and retreats; and loving community members of Interfaith Community Church, whose dedication to interfaith ideals has inspired me to become a more complete Muslim.

Credits

Scripture quotations in Rabbi Ted Falcon's sections are based on the author's translations, unless marked "JPS." Quotations marked "JPS" come from the *Hebrew-English Tanakh* (Philadelphia, PA: Jewish Publication Society, 1999). Translations of the Hebrew prayers are by Rabbi Ted Falcon.

Qur'an quotations in Sheikh Jamal Rahman's sections are from *The Holy Qur'an*: *Original Arabic Text with English Translation & Selected Commentaries*, by Abdullah Yusuf Ali (Kuala Lumpur, Malaysia: Saba Islamic Media, 2000), unless otherwise marked. The quotations marked "trans. Asad" are from *The Message of the Qu'ran*, translated and explained by Muhammad Asad, 2003, originally published by The Book Foundation, Watsonville, CA. The quotation marked "trans. A. A. Maududi" is from *Towards Understanding the Quran* by Abul Ala Maududi (New Delhi, India: Markazi Maktaba Islami Publishers, 2006). The quotation marked "trans. Ahmed Ali" is from *Al-Quran* by Ahmed Ali (Princeton, NJ: Princeton University Press, 1988).

The quotation marked "trans. Helminski" is from *The Light of Dawn: A Daybook of Verses from the Holy Qur'an*, selected and rendered by Camille Helminski, 1998, originally published by Threshold Books, Boston.

The photo on p. 112 is © 2005 by Don Mackenzie, Ted Falcon and Jamal Rahman.

Spirituality

Next to Godliness: Finding the Sacred in Housekeeping
Edited and with Introductions by Alice Peck
Offers new perspectives on how we can reach out for the Divine.
6 x 9, 224 pp, Quality PB, 978-1-59473-214-0 **$19.99**

Bread, Body, Spirit: Finding the Sacred in Food
Edited and with Introductions by Alice Peck
Explores how food feeds our faith. 6 x 9, 224 pp, Quality PB, 978-1-59473-242-3 **$19.99**

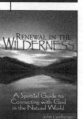

Renewal in the Wilderness: A Spiritual Guide to Connecting with God
in the Natural World *by John Lionberger*
Reveals the power of experiencing God's presence in many variations of the natural world. 6 x 9, 176 pp, b/w photos, Quality PB, 978-1-59473-219-5 **$16.99**

Honoring Motherhood: Prayers, Ceremonies and Blessings
Edited and with Introductions by Lynn L. Caruso
Journey through the seasons of motherhood. 5 x 7¼, 272 pp, HC, 978-1-59473-239-3 **$19.99**

Soul Fire: Accessing Your Creativity *by Rev. Thomas Ryan, CSP*
Learn to cultivate your creative spirit. 6 x 9, 160 pp, Quality PB, 978-1-59473-243-0 **$16.99**

Technology & Spirituality: How the Information Revolution Affects Our
Spiritual Lives *by Stephen K. Spyker* 6 x 9, 176 pp, HC, 978-1-59473-218-8 **$19.99**

Money and the Way of Wisdom: Insights from the Book of Proverbs
by Timothy J. Sandoval, PhD 6 x 9, 192 pp, Quality PB, 978-1-59473-245-4 **$16.99**

Awakening the Spirit, Inspiring the Soul
30 Stories of Interspiritual Discovery in the Community of Faiths
Edited by Brother Wayne Teasdale and Martha Howard, MD; Foreword by Joan Borysenko, PhD
6 x 9, 224 pp, HC, 978-1-59473-039-9 **$21.99**

Creating a Spiritual Retirement: A Guide to the Unseen Possibilities in Our Lives
by Molly Srode 6 x 9, 208 pp, b/w photos, Quality PB, 978-1-59473-050-4 **$14.99**
HC, 978-1-893361-75-1 **$19.95**

Finding Hope: Cultivating God's Gift of a Hopeful Spirit
by Marcia Ford 8 x 8, 200 pp, Quality PB, 978-1-59473-211-9 **$16.99**

The Geography of Faith: Underground Conversations on Religious, Political and Social
Change *by Daniel Berrigan and Robert Coles* 6 x 9, 224 pp, Quality PB, 978-1-893361-40-9 **$16.95**

Jewish Spirituality: A Brief Introduction for Christians *by Lawrence Kushner*
5½ x 8½, 112 pp, Quality PB, 978-1-58023-150-3 **$12.95** *(A book from Jewish Lights, SkyLight Paths' sister imprint)*

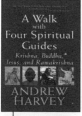

Journeys of Simplicity: Traveling Light with Thomas Merton, Bashō, Edward Abbey,
Annie Dillard & Others *by Philip Harnden*
5 x 7¼, 144 pp, Quality PB, 978-1-59473-181-5 **$12.99** 128 pp, HC, 978-1-893361-76-8 **$16.95**

Keeping Spiritual Balance As We Grow Older: More than 65 Creative Ways to
Use Purpose, Prayer, and the Power of Spirit to Build a Meaningful Retirement
by Molly and Bernie Srode 8 x 8, 224 pp, Quality PB, 978-1-59473-042-9 **$16.99**

Spirituality 101: The Indispensable Guide to Keeping—or Finding—Your Spiritual Life
on Campus *by Harriet L. Schwartz, with contributions from college students at nearly thirty campuses across the United States* 6 x 9, 272 pp, Quality PB, 978-1-59473-000-9 **$16.99**

A Walk with Four Spiritual Guides: Krishna, Buddha, Jesus, and Ramakrishna
by Andrew Harvey 5½ x 8½, 192 pp, 10 b/w photos & illus., Quality PB, 978-1-59473-138-9 **$15.99**

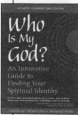

Who Is My God?, 2nd Edition: An Innovative Guide to Finding Your Spiritual Identity
Created by the Editors at SkyLight Paths 6 x 9, 160 pp, Quality PB, 978-1-59473-014-6 **$15.99**

Judaism / Christianity / Interfaith

Talking about God: Exploring the Meaning of Religious Life with Kierkegaard, Buber, Tillich and Heschel *by Daniel F. Polish, PhD*
Examines the meaning of the human religious experience with the greatest theologians of modern times. 6 x 9, 176 pp, HC, 978-1-59473-230-0 **$21.99**

Interactive Faith: The Essential Interreligious Community-Building Handbook
Edited by Rev. Bud Heckman with Rori Picker Neiss A guide to the key methods and resources of the interfaith movement. 6 x 9, 304 pp, HC, 978-1-59473-237-9 **$40.00**

The Jewish Approach to Repairing the World (*Tikkun Olam*)
A Brief Introduction for Christians *by Rabbi Elliot N. Dorff, PhD, with Reverend Cory Willson*
A window into the Jewish idea of responsibility to care for the world.
5½ x 8½, 256 pp, Quality PB, 978-1-58023-349-1 **$16.99** *(A book from Jewish Lights, SkyLight Paths' sister imprint)*

Modern Jews Engage the New Testament: Enhancing Jewish Well-Being in a Christian Environment *by Rabbi Michael J. Cook, PhD*
A look at the dynamics of the New Testament. 6 x 9, 416 pp, HC, 978-1-58023-313-2 **$29.99** *(A book from Jewish Lights, SkyLight Paths' sister imprint)*

Disaster Spiritual Care: Practical Clergy Responses to Community, Regional and National Tragedy
Edited by Rabbi Stephen B. Roberts, BCJC, & Rev. Willard W.C. Ashley, Sr., DMin, DH
The definitive reference for pastoral caregivers of all faiths involved in disaster response.
6 x 9, 384 pp, Hardcover, 978-1-59473-240-9 **$40.00**

The Changing Christian World: A Brief Introduction for Jews
by Rabbi Leonard A. Schoolman 5½ x 8½, 176 pp, Quality PB, 978-1-58023-344-6 **$16.99**
(A book from Jewish Lights, SkyLight Paths' sister imprint)

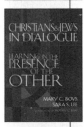

The Jewish Connection to Israel, the Promised Land: A Brief Introduction for Christians *by Rabbi Eugene Korn, PhD* 5½ x 8½, 192 pp, Quality PB, 978-1-58023-318-7 **$14.99**
(A book from Jewish Lights, SkyLight Paths' sister imprint)

Christians and Jews in Dialogue: Learning in the Presence of the Other
by Mary C. Boys and Sara S. Lee; Foreword by Dorothy C. Bass Inspires renewed commitment to dialogue between religious traditions. 6 x 9, 240 pp, HC, 978-1-59473-144-0 **$21.99**

Healing the Jewish-Christian Rift: Growing Beyond Our Wounded History
by Ron Miller and Laura Bernstein; Foreword by Dr. Beatrice Bruteau
6 x 9, 288 pp, Quality PB, 978-1-59473-139-6 **$18.99**

Introducing My Faith and My Community: The Jewish Outreach Institute Guide for the Christian in a Jewish Interfaith Relationship *by Rabbi Kerry M. Olitzky* 6 x 9, 176 pp, Quality PB, 978-1-58023-192-3 **$16.99** *(A book from Jewish Lights, SkyLight Paths' sister imprint)*

The Jewish Approach to God: A Brief Introduction for Christians *by Rabbi Neil Gillman*
5½ x 8½, 192 pp, Quality PB, 978-1-58023-190-9 **$16.95** *(A book from Jewish Lights, SkyLight Paths' sister imprint)*

Jewish Holidays: A Brief Introduction for Christians *by Rabbi Kerry M. Olitzky and Rabbi Daniel Judson* 5½ x 8½, 176 pp, Quality PB, 978-1-58023-302-6 **$16.99**
(A book from Jewish Lights, SkyLight Paths' sister imprint)

Jewish Ritual: A Brief Introduction for Christians
by Rabbi Kerry M. Olitzky and Rabbi Daniel Judson 5½ x 8½, 144 pp, Quality PB, 978-1-58023-210-4 **$14.99**
(A book from Jewish Lights, SkyLight Paths' sister imprint)

Jewish Spirituality: A Brief Introduction for Christians *by Rabbi Lawrence Kushner*
5½ x 8½, 112 pp, Quality PB, 978-1-58023-150-3 **$12.95** *(A book from Jewish Lights, SkyLight Paths' sister imprint)*

A Jewish Understanding of the New Testament *by Rabbi Samuel Sandmel;*
new Preface by Rabbi David Sandmel 5½ x 8½, 368 pp, Quality PB, 978-1-59473-048-1 **$19.99**

We Jews and Jesus: Exploring Theological Differences for Mutual Understanding
by Rabbi Samuel Sandmel; new Preface by Rabbi David Sandmel A Classic Reprint
6 x 9, 192 pp, Quality PB, 978-1-59473-208-9 **$16.99**

Show Me Your Way: The Complete Guide to Exploring Interfaith Spiritual Direction
by Howard A. Addison 5½ x 8½, 240 pp, Quality PB, 978-1-893361-41-6 **$16.95**

About SKYLIGHT PATHS Publishing

SkyLight Paths Publishing is creating a place where people of different spiritual traditions come together for challenge and inspiration, a place where we can help each other understand the mystery that lies at the heart of our existence.

Through spirituality, our religious beliefs are increasingly becoming a part of our lives—rather than *apart* from our lives. While many of us may be more interested than ever in spiritual growth, we may be less firmly planted in traditional religion. Yet, we do want to deepen our relationship to the sacred, to learn from our own as well as from other faith traditions, and to practice in new ways.

SkyLight Paths sees both believers and seekers as a community that increasingly transcends traditional boundaries of religion and denomination—people wanting to learn from each other, *walking together, finding the way.*

For your information and convenience, at the back of this book we have provided a list of other SkyLight Paths books you might find interesting and useful. They cover the following subjects:

Buddhism / Zen	Global Spiritual	Monasticism
Catholicism	Perspectives	Mysticism
Children's Books	Gnosticism	Poetry
Christianity	Hinduism /	Prayer
Comparative	Vedanta	Religious Etiquette
Religion	Inspiration	Retirement
Current Events	Islam / Sufism	Spiritual Biography
Earth-Based	Judaism	Spiritual Direction
Spirituality	Kabbalah	Spirituality
Enneagram	Meditation	Women's Interest
	Midrash Fiction	Worship

Or phone, fax, mail or e-mail to: SKYLIGHT PATHS Publishing
Sunset Farm Offices, Route 4 • P.O. Box 237 • Woodstock, Vermont 05091
Tel: (802) 457-4000 • Fax: (802) 457-4004 • www.skylightpaths.com
Credit card orders: (800) 962-4544 (8:30AM–5:30PM ET Monday–Friday)
Generous discounts on quantity orders. SATISFACTION GUARANTEED. Prices subject to change.